SCOOTERMANIA

SCOOTERMANIA

Josh Sims

C
CONWAY
BLOOMSBURY
LONDON · NEW DELHI · NEW YORK · SYDNEY

Published by Conway

An imprint of Bloomsbury Publishing Plc

www.bloomsbury.com

50 Bedford Square   1385 Broadway
London   New York
WC1B 3DP   NY 10018
UK   USA

First published 2015

British Library Cataloguing-in-Publication Data

A catalogue record for this book is available from the British Library.

ISBN: HB: 978-1-8448-6277-1
ePDF: 978-1-8448-6279-5
ePub: 978-1-8448-6278-8

10 9 8 7 6 5 4 3 2 1

Design by Nicola Liddiard at Nimbus Design

Printed in China

To find out more about our authors and books visit www.bloomsbury.com.
Here you will find extracts, author interviews, details of forthcoming
events and the option to sign up for our newsletters.

Contents

CHAPTER 1

History and design

In terms of public image, the scooter has long played second fiddle to the motorcycle. If the motorcycle – in large part due to Hollywood myth-making, from *The Wild One* to *Easy Rider* – suggested the romance of the open road, the scooter suggested another breakdown at the side of the road; if the motorcycle suggested the machismo of the outlaw figure, the scooter, in contrast, at times suggested prissiness and the feminine; if the motorcycle suggested power, the scooter suggested pootling, even at full throttle. The scooter is all small wheels and pop colours. The scooter is fun.

Of course, there is a large dose of stereotype in the readings of both kinds of machines and at heart both have provided the same thing: escape, independence, mobility and a certain kind of cool. Indeed, while, over its post-Second World War boom times the scooter has attained a smaller global following than the motorcycle, arguably it has inspired a more ardent following, especially given the relatively tiny – and often troubled – industry extant to supply it. It has perhaps also inspired more affection among the general public, precisely for its smallness, in scale, noise and attitude. Scooters can be cute. Even their name – 'scooters' – sounds cute, with, similarly,

A vintage scooter in a village square in Lazio, Italy, perhaps the nation where the scooter has been most at home.

the dominant companies behind them, most famously Piaggio with the Vespa and Innocenti with the Lambretta, suggesting a foreign exoticism and Italian chic, one that thankfully has survived globalisation.

Not, for sure, that these were the only manufacturers – and not by a long way. While longevity and pop culture have ensured that these two names have become bywords for the scooter – even generic terms akin to 'Hoover' for all kinds of vacuum cleaners – many other companies were involved in scooter production. The scene was set with much of Europe on the long road to post-war reconstruction, rationing still in place and cars unaffordable to buy and expensive to run for many – which is perhaps one reason why scooters generally failed to catch on in consumer booming America. Such was their expected appeal in the 1950s particularly that even motorcycle manufacturers dipped their toe in the waters.

One of the most attractive, and, it must be said, Vespa-like, designs of the 1950s, for example, was the British-made 175cc or 250cc Triumph Tigress. Its feminised name hinted at the market that Triumph perhaps had in mind. 'Tiger' would have been far too macho applied to a scooter. In 1952, even future

'super-bike' manufacturer Ducati produced a scooter, the rather more sexily named Cruiser. Ducatis, naturally, packed more power than most, housing an overhead-valve 175cc engine.

Yet throughout the scooter's history, its most successful variants have been designed and built by specialists. And, it might be added, attracted a specialist audience, too, who understood and appreciated that a scooter was not a poor cousin to the motorcycle, but something altogether different: progressive, modernistic, accessible and fashionable.

New wheels
THE FIRST GENERATION

While the scooter may be most readily associated with the names Vespa and Lambretta and the story of Italy's post-war social and industrial restoration, its history is much older and deeper. Indeed, the decades immediately following the Second World War are often characterised by historians of transport as the scooter's second wave, the first dating back to 1916, when a roughly 10-year period saw the first vehicles of this kind take to the streets – and sometimes successfully. Many of the manufacturers who created, and later developed, the scooter market hailed from the aviation industry, and used their technical knowhow in one field of advanced engineering to create another. Arguably, it was not being hidebound by the rules of automobile design that allowed them to be so inventive.

Certainly the first wave was a boldly inventive time, both mechanically and stylistically, in large part because, unlike the motorcycle – which was by this time established in both form and intention – the scooter was genuinely new. It was not merely a motorised bicycle (one basic distinction between scooter and moped is that it is only the latter than retains pedals), but a fresh form of mobility entirely, most widely characterised by having a step-through

US postmen, pictured here in 1917, with an early version of the scooter.

body. The result was that, within that general characterisation, these early years of the scooter witnessed both a huge diversity of looks and new approaches to engineering. Most notably, this was the first time that motors would be developed especially for the machines, whereas typically a new design of motorcycle would be built around a pre-existing power plant.

The very first scooter might be said to date from an earlier century. In 1894 Munich-based Hildebrand & Wolfmüller launched a two-wheeled, two-cylinder, four-stroke, motorised vehicle with an open frame design that could lay claim to being a scooter. Made in Germany and at a second plant in France, the H&W sold well for what would have been considered a radical proposition at the time.

Hildebrand and
Wolfmuller's petrol
motor bicycle, first
patented in 1894.

Some 20 years later the market opened up considerably, with several manufacturers setting up to launch scooters, and established makers of cars and even aircraft also building models. The breadth and quality of design varied wildly, some seemingly the work of amateurs, which only served to put off an initially intrigued and then wary public. The British-made Stafford Pup, for instance, made by the company that would go on to produce Alvis cars, placed almost the entire weight of its (admittedly advanced) engine to the left of the front wheel, which made precision steering hazardous.

But each new model invariably proposed some new idea – not to mention a typically fantastic name, such as the Autoglider or the Reynolds Runabout – also British – that might contribute to the mid-twentieth-century notion of a classic scooter. The bestseller of the period, the Skootamota, may have been marketed during the 1920s as the ideal runabout for those streamlined-attired, progressive young ladies that went by the name of flappers, and it did come with a sunshade, no less, advancing the notion that a scooter should protect the rider. Such scooters did not have wide appeal but they did represent steps in scooter evolution.

In the UK, the Autoped of 1916, for instance, which is more often cited than the H&W as the world's first scooter, was more akin to a child's scooter, sized for grown-ups: it was ridden standing up and had a clever steering column that, pushed forward, engaged power and, pulled back, applied the brake. Hopeful of strong demand, its maker's advertising coined a new verb in its slogan: 'Autopeding – something new in transportation'. The Autoglider of 1920, meanwhile, looked nothing less than a lawn mower engine mounted on a plate between two wheels but, given that it did have a seat, was marketed as offering 'the maximum amount of comfort and reliability for the minimum expenditure'. Even in their infancy scooters were promoted on their relative good economy.

Arguably the most important scooter of the period was the radical and futuristic Unibus, also of 1920. This was produced by the Gloucester Aircraft Company and designed by Harold Boultebee. For all that it was priced way out of most people's reach – over £99, relative to the Autoglider's 55 guineas – it was the first scooter design with a fully enclosed body. With the almost futuristic style that Boultebee gave to the Unibus – a curvy front windshield,

Left: A 1920 advertisement for Harold Boultebee's Unibus scooter.

Below: An early 1920s French poster emphasised the scooter's appeal to women.

channel-section frame and left-spring suspension – he might well be said to have been the stylistic forebear of Corradino D'Ascanio, the helicopter designer who would create the first Vespa over 20 years later – the model that for many defines today's conception of what a scooter is.

Boultebee's design afforded its rider a new level of protection from the elements, and its engine, vertically mounted behind the front wheel – another innovation – provided stability. Unfortunately it was too late (and too expensive) to appease an already sceptical public, and by the early years of the 1920s interest in the scooter was rapidly fading. If only the Unibus had come a little earlier, and at a cheaper price, the 1920s and 30s, rather than the 1950s and

60s, might now be regarded as the scooter's golden era. And a British, rather than an Italian golden era to boot. Some historians of the scooter have dismissed its first wave as little more than a passing fad – a fashion no more and no less than bobbed hair and Art Deco style, and destined to become outmoded just as quickly, although in the scooter's case ably assisted by the rapid rise of the car.

Right wheels
THE SECOND GENERATION

In time, fashion would become the scooter's lifeforce. But first it would take a radical reappraisal of what the scooter was and who it was for to find its market. This proved to be just about anyone looking for a simple, reliable, stylish means of transportation rather than the almost exclusively male, greasy-handed, garage tinkering enthusiast. It was, in other words, less a product of amateur mechanics and more one of progressive lifestyle. Indeed, as the late Eric Brockway, one of the managers of the Douglas Vespa business (of which more later) noted, 'the first to be won over by the new mode of transport were, in the main, the professional classes – no young person in a 'better off' society would consider him or herself complete without a Vespa. A motor car was out of the reach of most young people, so the Vespa scooter took its place'.

If the scooter has a public image – especially among non-scooterists – it is a deeply Italian one. Indeed, for some the scooter is as Italian as cappuccino, another of the country's successful exports. And with good reason: if the rush to market of the late 1910s had seen some 18 different manufacturers enter the fray with a scooter in the space of just two years (few of them completely

MOTOR CYCLING   *November 15, 1951.*

ALWAYS THE CENTRE OF ATTRACTION THROUGHOUT THE WORLD.

Douglas

Vespa 125cc

THE TWO WHEEL CAR

OWN A VESPA & ENJOY TRAVEL INDEPENDENCE

STAND No. 9 MAIN HALL

DOUGLAS (SALES AND SERVICE) LTD., KINGSWOOD, BRISTOL

The fresh, clean advertising used by Douglas Vespa reflected the professional market they were aiming to capture.

Amelia Earhart,
the legendary
aviator, on a
motorised
scooter.

competently executed), initially just two major players rose to the challenge in the post-Second World War years. As they did so, they reinvented the scooter as dependable, easy to maintain, easy to ride, affordable, accessible and – something previous manufacturers had never made much capital of – fun.

But the Italians were not quite there first. Surprisingly, for what is generally considered to be a deeply European phenomenon, some have attributed the breakthrough moment to the United States, more specifically Oakland, California – where the weather at least was good for riding. There, in 1935, E. Foster Salsbury had seen the pioneering aviator and feminist icon Amelia Earhart pottering around Burbank's Lockheed Airport on a Motoped – little more than a motorised stand-up-style scooter. And that, as he would later say, 'got me starting thinking about building a real scooter'. The prototype of his Motor Glide was revealed in 1936, and by the end of the year had inspired versions from several other companies such as Rock-Ola, Zip Scoot, Construct-scoot, Moto-Scoot and Cushman; and this despite scooter manufacturers there facing the uphill climb of a market in which the car was relatively affordable.

Moto-Scoot's founder Norman Siegal was declared by *Time* magazine – a little pre-emptively as it turned out – to be the 'Henry Ford of the scooter business', such were his sales in the closing years of the 1930s. But the company would shift the focus of its manufacturing following the US entry into the Second World War, and never went back to scooters. Cushman and Salsbury, however, did well at home during the war. Not only were the raw materials needed to make and run cars in short supply, so the idea of scooter-riding gained popularity, but the US War Department granted both companies rights to sell to the general public (see below). Naturally enough, the American consumer market – already on its way to its post-war boom times – would not stand for a humdrum utilitarian vehicle. Salsbury's Model 72 could not only be accessorised with windshields and sidecars, seats and electric horns, it came in a range of custom colours.

But the appeal of Salsbury's scooters went deeper. Quite why Salsbury's machines proved so influential is easy to fathom when one considers the fact that it was his models which introduced the idea of automatic transmission, or the 'self-shifting torque

**Screen legend
Rita Hayworth on
a Motor Glide
scooter in 1941.**

converter' as the company somewhat inelegantly referred to it; an idea, indeed, that is found at the mechanical heart of almost every scooter built today. More than this, Salsbury had taken the time to consider precisely what a scooter had to be in order to fill the gap in the market.

It needed a step-through chassis, so women wearing skirts could ride it as easily as those wearing trousers (the idea that women would prove a crucial market for the scooter had been suggested back in 1910, when a three-wheeled scooter, the Moto Frip, was designed and launched by Mrs Olive Kent in the UK). The bodywork had to be shaped in order to protect the rider from the engine and the elements; consequently the motor also needed to be not only small, but tucked away, close to the rear wheel. And transmission needed to be automatic – the scooter had to be easy to ride. Just about every successful scooter that followed adhered to many if not all of these tenets. Only the US entry into the Second World War, and a consequent change of emphasis for heavy manufacturing and engineering, perhaps prevented the Motor Glide from becoming the cult object for generations to follow.

Into BATTLE

The Second World War placed its own requirements on scooter design. Salsbury sold some of its standard Model 72s to the US Navy for transportation around bases – and also produced an ambulance version – and the company was actually acquired by a defence contractor by the war's end.

A specialist product was required for dropping out of aircraft. In 1943 the US government put out a tender for production of a lightweight scooter to be used as an airborne vehicle, providing paratroopers with an on-the-spot means of transportation when they landed. The idea was already in play: Volugrafo Aermoto made a scooter for the Italian forces and Welbike made a folding scooter for the British forces. This latter vehicle took its name from Welwyn, the British town where the Research and Design Establishment of the Special Operations Executive (SOE) was located, and where the Welmine, Welgun and Welman one-man submarine were also developed. The Welbike, weighing in at just 70 pounds and with a 90-mile range, was designed so as to fit into a cylinder just 6 feet long and 15 inches in diameter, and to be assembled on landing in as short a time as possible – officially in 11 seconds. Its manufacturer, Excelsior, took the first order in 1942

Top: The Excelsior Welbike could be put together in just seconds.

Below: US troops assemble a Welbike on the battlefield.

The Cushman Airborne scooter had tyres that were interchangeable with aircraft.

and the last in the summer of 1943, during which time some 3,600 were made, very few of which actually saw combat. Neither did the other folding bikes designed to be used in war zones, such as James' so-called Clockwork Mouse and Royal Enfield's Flying Flea. In fact, the two-wheeled vehicle most typically seen in action for the British was a BSA-made bicycle.

The battle for the US contract, meanwhile, fell between Cushman Motor Works, which quickly assembled a prototype of what it called its Model 53, and Cooper Motors of Los Angeles, which proposed its more nattily named Cooper Combat Motor Scooter. A natty name, however, was not enough. Cooper's factory was deemed sub par and the

contract went to the more reliable Cushman, which proceeded to make some 4,000 Model 53s, effectively a stripped-back civilian scooter, by the end of the war. The scooter saw action on D-Day, as well as in the Mediterranean and Pacific theatres. Unlike the many custom colours demanded by civilian consumers, the Model 53 was available in just two: olive drab, for obvious reasons of camouflage, and bright yellow, to be seen easily on an airfield for example. Consumers would not have stood for its other basic qualities either: no lighting and no suspension. One clever aspect of its design, however, had been to fit the Model 53 with 6-inch tyres that were interchangeable with those used on the air force's spotter aircraft.

The bold design of the Salsbury Model 85 was a welcome antidote to wartime austerity.

Rather than redesign or upgrade the Model 53, after the war Cushman simply added back a few accessories it has first stripped away, jazzed it up with a less grim or garish paint job and called it a 'family scooter' – and sold plenty to an enthusiastic public. For a while at least: the Model 53 soon began to look rather paltry next to, for example, the Model 85, from Cushman's great rival Salsbury. Rather than continue with wartime limitations, the Model 85 was a bold, vibrant reaction against them, all comfort, go faster stripes and futuristic curves. This was the scooter of tomorrow – one of the first road vehicles to be tested in a wind tunnel, no less – for a consumer who, for a time at least, was ready to embrace understated two-wheeled transport.

The honour of pioneering post-war design, however fell predominantly to two Italian manufacturers, although there were also many scooter makers in West Germany, the UK, Spain and further afield. It was these two firms that helped further refine Salsbury's idea of the scooter as simplicity on two wheels, introducing the notion – a notion that spread like wildfire – of the scooter as an approachable tool to enhance both your social life and living standards. Or, in others words, as both a useful form of transport and a kind of fashion accessory, one which would chime perfectly with the post-war period's burgeoning mass entertainment of movieland and the rise of this newfangled thing called youth culture.

Vespa
KING OF CURVES

These two manufacturers, Innocenti, based out of Milan, and Piaggio, based out of Pontedera, near Pisa, had, of course, the benefit of much-improved manufacturing technology, thanks to the rapid advances necessarily wrought by the war effort of many nations. But they also had incentive: as a condition of surrender, Axis nations' heavy industry was banned from making anything for obvious military use (which, strictly speaking, did not discount the scooter, but that did not seem to bother the authorities), so they had to find products they could make that would both keep their work force in employment and the business alive.

Equally, if not more importantly, they also had a ready market – a people unable to afford to own or run a car, a shattered public transport infrastructure, severely bomb-damaged roads but, overriding all of this, still a need for the populace to get around. Italy even benefited from a lack of history in scootering. While in Britain scooters had long failed to shed their reputation as novelty items, on the Continent no such preconceptions existed. Add in Italy's warmer climate and the country may be thought of as an ideal home for the scooter's second wave.

Above: A Vespa is dropped by balloon at the 1957 Milan Sample Fair.

Right: Enrico Piaggio spearheaded his firm's development of a vehicle for the masses.

The first to market in Italy was Piaggio, previously an aircraft manufacturer, but now, like so many of the manufacturers behind the post-war scooter boom, in need of a civilian product to sell. Like the Gloucester Aircraft Company before with its Unibus, but this time with the zeitgeist on its side, Piaggio's second attempt at a scooter model, the Vespa – Italian for 'wasp', in part for its waisted shape, in part for the buzz of its engine – was almost perfect straight off its designer's sketchpad, with consequent models over many years offering only cosmetic changes or advances in engine performance or power.

Almost, at least. There had been bumps in the road. The 'Vespa' name had already been given by aircraft-turned-motorbike manufacturer MV Augusta to one of its models, sparking a race to register the name first, which Piaggio won. Then there was the close escape when Piaggio attempted to market the new design under the Moto Guzzi name, an approach the latter company rejected on the grounds that it saw no future in scooters. Then there was Piaggio's duff first attempt that preceded the Vespa...

Enrico Piaggio had taken control of his father's huge company in, as bad luck would have it, 1938, just a year before Italy found itself at war. Societa

'Transport for the people'? A gleaming Vespa from 1946.

Anonima Piaggio had been founded by Rinaldo Piaggio in 1884, making woodworking machinery, then rolling stock, cars and aircraft – for the latter it can be credited with the invention of both the pressurised cabin and the retractable landing gear. During the Second World War it had built Italy's only heavy bomber, the P-108. That, of course, was one thing it could not continue to make after the war, quite aside from the fact that its factories had been destroyed. 'Our over 10,000 employees were thrown out of work by the bombings and by the fact that, as soon as the war was over, our production fell to zero,' Enrico Piaggio said some 12 years later. 'In fact, we were prohibited from making airplanes by the peace treaty. So you see it was essential that we find a new peacetime product for the sake of the Piaggio company and our employees.'

Enrico had already considered the potential in a civilian version of the war scooter devised by Volugrafo Aermoto well before the war's end (car company Fiat had even prototyped a scooter before the war had started, back in 1938, but decided not to take the idea forward) and so assigned engineers Vittorio Casini and Renzo Spolti to design one. Dubbed the MP5 or, in more friendly fashion, the

New models on the Douglas stand at Earls Court in 1946.

Paperino – 'small duck', after Disney's Donald Duck – the first attempt disregarded what Salsbury had identified a decade before: that a step-through frame made it a vehicle with appeal to women. It was not a looker either. Enrico would comment that the Paperino was 'a horrible looking thing', noting that 'people ridiculed us to our faces'. Time, he thought, to start again from scratch and hire some outside inspiration, namely Corradino D'Ascanio, helicopter designer, a man who was perhaps so free-thinking in his approach precisely because he had never designed a two-wheeled vehicle before. 'I drew a man sitting down comfortably, with wheels beneath him [and] immediately a design was born', as he is said to have put it nonchalantly.

The result, initially referred to just as the MP6, certainly offered an aesthetic improvement. The first, 98cc Vespas – just 100 of them, each looking like some kind of rocket bike ridden by a Dan Dare or a Flash Gordon – rolled off the production line in 1945 and made their debut in early 1946 to a private audience at the Rome Golf Club and, a few weeks later, their public debut at the Milan Spring Fair. Incredibly, by the end of the year Piaggio had sold almost 2,500 of them. And within five years – notably

Douglas produced Vespas such as this under licence from Piaggio but found it hard to maintain the production levels required.

after some minor improvements introduced in 1947 to effectively create the Vespa look best known today – they were being sold all over the world. A decade after its launch, in April 1956, the one millionth Vespa was made (already a quarter of all the scooters that would ever be made by rival Innocenti) prompting major street parties in 15 cities across Italy – including a 2,000 scooter-strong convoy through Rome – on what was declared to be Vespa Day. Just shy of three decades later and Piaggio would have sold some 7.25 million Vespas.

Such was demand for the Vespa that they were even being made under licence in Germany by the likes of Hoffman and Messerschmitt (makers of the Second World War's famed Me109 fighter aeroplane), as far afield as Chile, by Spencer & Cio, and in Spain by a Vespa subsidiary. In the UK, Bristol-based truck and engine manufacturer Douglas was in the hands of the official receiver in 1948 and facing closure when its new managing director, Claude McCormack, had his first sighting of a scooter while on holiday in Italy. He knew he had found a way out for the company if only he could win the licence from Piaggio, which he did. This was not without its attendant risks, not least because of Britain's strong

heritage in motorcycles and the fact that the market remained largely perplexed as to just what this newfangled scooter contraption was actually for. A headline in the *Daily Mail*, a major British national newspaper, summed it up: 'Big Show Surprise – Britain to make Italian midget motorcycle'.

But Douglas overcame the naysayers and their Vespas were, from 1951, the first to be sold in Britain – prompting Modish desire in the process – and, come 1959, half of the new two-wheeled vehicles sold in the UK were scooters. The Douglas Vespa, with many of its parts British-made, also encouraged the introduction of one lasting design improvement: the original Vespa had its headlight placed on the front mudguard, where it was prone to get dirty and become somewhat ineffective; British lighting regulations would not allow that, so the headlight was set higher up on the front apron, nearer the handlebars, and then on the handlebars themselves. The idea fed back to Piaggio and stuck.

But at the core of the Vespa design was the aircraft-inspired monocoque – or one-piece, pressed steel – bodywork, which, relative to the steel box or tubular frame construction typical of the 1910s and 20s, gave the scooter a lightness without sacrificing

Right: The
scooter was a
perfect form of
transport young
people at their
leisure.

Opposite: City
workers also
found it an
efficient means
of getting
around town.

integral strength, qualities that other manufacturers were attempting to achieve through the use of sheet aluminium or fibreglass. 'Here too,' as D'Ascanio would note, 'my experience in the field of aeronautics helped me, [since] in that field lightness of structure must not interfere with its sturdiness.'

This frame was also ahead of its time in being spot-welded, a practice now common in car and even racing motorbike manufacturing. Further details were borrowed from aircraft design: the stub axle front fork and solid dish wheels, for example. Remarkably – especially for the many subsequent generations of scooterists for whom their scooter is their pride and joy – D'Ascanio also neglected to give his Vespa design any kind of stand. It perhaps speaks to just how utilitarian, and replaceable, the Vespa was conceived as being in its homeland that to park it the rider just leaned it over on to the running board, or, indeed, just on to its side.

Perhaps more importantly to a country whose style industries were also experiencing their fledgling years, the monocoque construction also gave the Vespa smooth, distinctive, uninterrupted lines, perfect for decals or to show off colourful paintwork. D'Ascanio was not the only designer pursuing this monocoque idea: another Italian company, Moto Rumi, a maker of midget submarines turned short-lived scooter manufacturer, had designed a monocoque-based scooter made out of cast aluminium but then failed to pursue the idea.

However, it was D'Ascanio's, which he freely admitted was – taking Enrico's lead – inspired by the Aermoto, that was most complete; this in some part due to its simplicity, which allowed it to be manufactured more efficiently, and hence more profitably. Indeed, D'Ascanio (and his often unsung assistant Mario D'Este) set the pace – or, if you like, revived the attitude of the scooter's first wave – in making innovative design a scooter benchmark. While motorcycle design tended to revert to an essentially tried-and-tested traditional form and engineering, scooter design was frequently progressive.

Right from the outset of the MP6 project, D'Ascanio had identified a number of what might be called lifestyle issues he wished to resolve: for one, positioning the gear change on the handlebars, which made the scooter both more intuitive and manoeuvrable. An aspect of motorbikes he didn't like was that oil would get sprayed over the rider's

clothes, so he intended to move the engine back as far as possible from the 'pilot' – his telling word – and cover it with a fairing. This was as much because D'Ascanio from the outset realised that the scooter could prove a 'design object' as much as a means of transport, so fluid lines would be essential. And, with no chain to get in the way he made it quick and easy to change a tyre. As he put it himself, 'having witnessed motorcyclists stranded at the side of the road many times with a punctured tyre, I decided that one of the most important things to resolve was that a flat should no longer be a large problem just like it wasn't for automobiles.'

Certainly, for all of the scooter's reputation as a second-class citizen to the motorcycle, many of the ideas that would later be found on motorcycles originated on scooters, a product perhaps of the fact that, like the Vespa, many scooters were designed from scratch, with every component originated as required as the design developed. Shaft drive and direct-gear drive engineering, for example, were found on scooters just two years later, in 1947, while motorcycles clung on to temperamental and grubby chain drives. (In fairness to them, Piaggio only invented this direct-drive positioning because the

transmission belts being provided by Pirelli were not up to the job, high-quality rubber still being in short supply in Italy at the time.) Cable-controlled gear change was introduced by Piaggio in 1951, replacing the complex rod arrangement used in its models up until then. Disc brakes, similarly, had first been used on a Maserati motorcycle, but, as far as the first mass-production vehicle is concerned, were first used on Lambrettas in the 1960s. It took more than a decade for them to appear on the first mass-production motorcycles. Engines were mounted transversally for the first time, notably in Velocette's Viceroy; and water cooling, again, only found on motorcycles in the 1980s, was used on a scooter, from the French manufacturer PP Roussey, in 1954.

While motorcycles required additional panniers if any kind of luggage was to be carried, from the outset post-war scooter design made its machines practical: space was made available under the seat – enough, at least, to house a helmet – in panniers integral to the bodywork, or as part of the apron; in fact, just about any place where the bodywork could be left hollow. Most designs made a spare wheel integral too. Manufacturers were also smart to make scooters personal, providing them in a variety of

Top: With their scooter laden with camping gear this couple toured France in the 1950s.

Below: A variety of Vespa models, including various ways of towing a passenger, dating from the 1950s.

colours, together with any number of accessories, many of which were produced by quick-off-the-mark non-scooter manufacturers, to allow a mass-market product to become one's own individualised machine.

Piaggio in particular would play with this idea too: when it introduced its 145cc GS or Grand Sport model in 1955, it was soon rated by enthusiasts as the best performing scooter on the market, and went through some four further permutations over the next five years; the last, the VS5, remaining in production until 1963. But one thing united all of the GS models: they were only ever available in metallic silver grey. In this instance, colour, or, rather, the lack of choice in it, became a badge of cool.

Arguably, however, it was less about design, manufacturing or marketing skill that – unlike rival Innocenti – allowed Piaggio to survive as a company through an international collapse in demand for scooters during the 1970s and 80s – the fuel crises of the earlier decade excepted. That might be attributed to a more intimate event that took place quietly in 1959, when Enrico Piaggio's daughter Antonella and Umberto Agnelli, heir to the giant Fiat empire, got married, thus effectively uniting two Italian automotive powerhouses.

Lambretta
STREAMLINED DREAM

Ferdinando Innocenti faced much the same post-war restrictions and reconstruction problems as Enrico Piaggio. He had established the steel tubing company in 1922 in Rome (where in 1931 it would provide all of the drainage pipes for the gardens at the Papal residence of Castelgandolfino), later moving much of the company to the Milanese suburb of Lambrate. Here, along the Lambrate river that would later give his scooter its name, Innocenti's company expanded massively making bomb casings and aircraft hangers in anticipation of the war to come. Back in Rome, an Innocenti plant made some 40,000 bullets a day and was named a 'model fascist factory' by the Italian government. That, of course, was not to last.

Like Piaggio, scooter production seemed to be a way for the business to survive, although Innocenti and Piaggio are said to have started their respective scooter projects in complete ignorance of the other's intention. But while Innocenti began work on its first scooter as soon as Italy was liberated, in 1944, its first production scooter, the Model A, was not launched until the autumn of 1947, almost two years after the first Piaggio scooter.

If the occupying authorities had not been much more restrictive in Milan than in Pisa, Innocenti may not have lost so much ground to Piaggio. And it could so easily have been Innocenti who carried the day; the industrialist had, after all, met with Corradino D'Ascanio with a view to them working together on a scooter as soon as the war allowed. It was an alliance that never came to fruition. Then, although briefed to design a scooter based on the utilitarian Cushman Model 32, the designer hired in place of D'Ascanio took the streamlined shape of a torpedo as the inspiration for what was called Experiment O, Innocenti's prototype machine. He even proposed that it be made from the pressed steel then being used in aeronautical design. But, for reasons unknown – quite possibly because the conditions of war still did not allow it – the Experiment O was never put into production.

What eventually was put into production – some time after Innocenti had been advertising that it was 'Lambretta Time' – was very different. Certainly, everything the Vespa had – the futuristic curves, the design innovation – the first, Model A Lambretta, designed by Pier Luigi Torre, did not. There was no great style to it. There was no suspension – the sprung seat aside. And, since the engine was air-cooled, it was not hidden away to streamlined effect.

Top: The Lambretta 125cc Model A, first produced in 1947.   **Centre: The Model B (1948) had far better suspension.**   **Below: The Model C released in 1950 refined the design further.**

But what it lacked in sophistication, it made up for, like the Cushman scooters Innocenti admired, in build quality and engine size – a fan-less 125cc, necessitating that it be uncovered. In fact, among scooterists Lambretta always had the reputation for being the faster marque. Crucially, the first model also had a second seat, and the engine convinced that it could carry two passengers. Innocenti was also determined to make up lost ground through his production methods, being one of the first heavy industry operations in Europe to make use of Taylorism and American-style line assembly.

With the Model B and Model C that swiftly followed, all the downsides of the Model A disappeared, creating machines that were clearly on their way to matching the Vespa. The B brought in rear suspension and a twist-grip gear change. The C, introduced in 1950, brought in a better engine and completely new chassis. An LC version – with LC standing for 'lusso' or luxury – even had an enclosed engine and fan cooling. Lambretta certainly did not sit on its laurels. The following year saw the introduction of the D Series. Three years later the company introduced a model with the biggest scooter engine to date, at 148cc.

ROBIN SPALDING
the collector

You could say that Robin Spalding has the tendency to collect. 'I started collecting die-cast models when I was eight and until recently had hundreds and hundreds of them. Now I just have hundreds', says the retired engineer, scooter expert and author. 'I'm a born collector and get excited about the challenge of finding the next addition. I'm on the hunt. And I love the hunt, although it's much easier to do it with die-cast models than with scooters.'

That has not stopped him being spectacularly successful at it and over a relatively short time. Yes, he may have got his first scooter back in 1957, if only because his father banned him from owning a motorcycle. But that brief foray into two-wheels soon passed into a love of cars. 'When I had my Austin Ten and could take the girls out without getting wet in the rain, I was sold on cars,' he recalls. At least, that is, until 1999. He was having an extension to his house built when he proposed to his wife that 'it would be nice to have a vintage scooter in the corner of the room, as decoration, alongside the jukebox,' he says. 'There was a long pause before she replied but she went for it. And after I bought that first scooter, I found I had the space, money and inclination to buy more.'

But the more he learned about the history of scooters, the more something dawned on him: that the history of British-made scooters had not only gone undocumented, but was in danger of being lost to history altogether. 'In part that was because most people thought that the British hadn't done too well making scooters, or the things they did make that looked like scooters,' he explains. 'The British

SCOOTER
PARKING
ONLY

ALL OTHERS
WILL BE
CRUSHED

industry of the 1950s was far too late in addressing demand for scooters and when it did, typically took a [not always reliable] Villiers engine and then tried to build around it, so the result was a scooter than looked more like a motorcycle. The British had such a strong history in designing and making motorbikes that it was slightly snobbish about scooters. The makers invariably just wanted to make what they wanted to make – not what the customer wanted.'

Notwithstanding Spalding's notion that perhaps it was better if the British attempts at designing and selling scooters were left to history, he made it what he calls his 'mission' to collect only British ones. And in a big way: by the end of his frenzied searching he had 42 British-made scooters, which amounts to every model of British scooter ever made. He funded the collection in part by selling his Rolls Royce Silver Shadow, but also simply out of the sheer chutzpah of wanting to complete the set.

'Collecting was an expensive business but, as Mr Royce once said, the price is soon forgotten when one enjoys the quality of what one has purchased,' says Spalding. 'By then I also had a few continental scooters and they had to go. People couldn't understand why I was selling those beauties but they appreciated that building a collection of British scooters was a good thing to do. In the end they filled every square foot of my garage and a log cabin.'

In choosing to collect British scooters, Spalding had certainly set himself a mission: some were easy to find but hard to restore, with replacement parts having to be custom-made based on grainy photographs in old 1950s brochures and magazines (the makers long since having closed their business or lost any helpful archive material). Other scooters required little restoration but were hard to find, although he benefited from tip-offs from members of the Vintage Motor Scooter Club and similar organizations in the UK. The

last scooter he added to the collection was a model called the Ambassador, launched in 1960 in carnation pink paintwork, for the ladies – of which only 15 were made. He found that one on eBay.

'My fear was always that someone would come up with a one-of-a-kind scooter, or the last of its kind, and then demand a silly price for it,' says Spalding, 'even though there would have been hardly anyone who would want to buy it, especially if any restoration was required. Yet that never happened: most sellers were from the scooter world and admired the mission. They wanted to help out.'

The collection, however, finally outran itself, and Spalding. 'I was coming up to 70 years of age and was conscious of the hassle of disposing of the scooters that would fall to someone,' he says. So, after an exhibition of many of the scooters at the Coventry Transport Museum, in the UK, in 2012, fortuitously the following year he was approached by the British Motorcycle Charitable Trust to buy the collection. After the assistance of an expert from Bonham's, the London auction house, a price was agreed on.

'I'd been approached by auction houses before, but they would have broken up the collection, which I didn't want,' says Spalding. 'And on one occasion an American billionaire wanted to buy them all, but I wanted to keep these British scooters in Britain. So this arrangement was ideal.' The collection is to be displayed at Haynes International Motor Museum in Somerset. It will prove a revelation to anyone who thinks of scooters as only being of Italian stock.

'I do want people to understand that we in Britain did have a scooter industry,' says Spalding. 'Most people don't know that. But then even in their heyday British scooters were never very popular. You hardly ever saw one on the road, while you saw Vespas and Lambrettas in their thousands of course. The collection was an important reminder.'

Left: A Lambretta from 1959 that is significantly more streamlined than earlier models.

Right: Lambretta scooters being assembled at the Innocenti factory in 1963.

Indeed, it was the rapidity of the company's product development that, from 1957, saw it launch scooters that at last proved viable competition for the Vespa: the TV175 Series 1 (not widely considered a success, having been rushed to market and, after just 16 months, pulled from production), and the breakthrough Li150 and 125 models. These were the more angular, 'slimstyle' models, as one ad called them, with 'superb styling, superb features' that would so appeal to the equally streamlined Mod in the UK. As with Piaggio, international sales success came quickly, with manufacturing licensed out to the likes of NSU in West Germany and Siambretta in Argentina, with production also starting up in Spain and India.

Not that Lambretta was set on out-scootering Piaggio. Unlike Piaggio, Innocenti was never quite dependent on its scooters being sales successes. It continued to produce steel tubing, as well as components for much of the burgeoning Italian car industry, and also for Volkswagen, Ford and Austin (Innocenti even made the Italian version of the Mini in its entirety). But, perhaps, that additional production was not enough. Ferdinando Innocenti died in 1966, just as demand for scooters began to go into decline,

chiefly as rising affluence was convincing more and more people to switch to a car. His company's scooter business had been undergoing a slow demise for the previous four years, despite the launch of ever more swanky models. The year before, the British Motor Corporation had taken over effective control of the company and turned its tooling over to production of the Mini, figuring making the iconic car in Italy would add to its 'continental' appeal. It did – such that the BMC clearly saw its future in cars, not in scooters.

However, Innocenti's last hurrahs were impressive ones: the 'ink blot' GP range of 1968, styled by the Italian automobile designer Giuseppe Bertone, had an ink splash decal on the leg shield said to be in the spot where Bertone dropped an ink spot onto his drawing-board; and the GP200 Electronic of 1970, often regarded as one of the best Lambrettas ever. But come 1971, production of Lambrettas in Italy ground to a halt. It continued abroad, most notably in India, where scooter demand for a largely poor but aspirational population was still very high, and where the licensed manufacturer had bought up all the Italian tooling in 1972. And that was that for Lambretta. Three years later the industrialist

A worker at Lambretta loading finished scooters for distribution.

Alejandro de Tomaso bought the Milan factory for the production of the various motorcycle and car marques in his ownership. As if true to its notion that the scooter had no future, one of these was Moto Guzzi, the company that turned down the Vespa.

Dead donkeys
AND OTHER ITALIANS

Following Piaggio and Innocenti, gradually the scooter manufacturing base grew throughout the 1950s and 60s as demand came to be proven across Europe. Indeed, while Vespa and Lambretta are the names that have captured the public imagination, it would be misleading to suggest that the rise of the scooter was entirely down to them. Theirs may have been the greatest successes – in image as much as in production numbers – but certainly the 1950s in particular were rife with makers of ground-breaking, smartly engineered machines, the vast array of engineers behind each bringing their own special solutions to the challenges of scootering.

Even in Italy Piaggio and Innocenti were not alone. As the British journal *Motor Cycle* noted as early as 1950, scooters were rapidly becoming a distinctly Italian expertise. 'The factors which have caused their great popularity in Italy can be summed up as: elegance; convenience, public transport in Italian towns being a nightmare; extreme economy; cleanliness; remarkable reliability – to see a Vespa or Lambretta broken-down is about as common as the sight of a dead donkey; and such conveniences as an easily changed spare wheel and the possibility of carrying the whole family in one way or another'.

The perfect vehicle for sightseeing: US sailors on scooters in Rome in 1954.

Right: Released in 1952, the Ducati Cruiser was designed as a luxury scooter.

Opposite: The Rumi 215cc 'Tipo Sport' scooter, 1960. Rumis were reputed to be the fastest scooters in production.

Certainly to see several people piled onto a single scooter was not uncommon at the time. It also helped that in Italy scooters were exempt from registration or taxation.

Small wonder MV Augusta, best known as a motorbike manufacturer, also dabbled in scooters, with its Ovunque – meaning 'everywhere' – best remembered for the innovative single-shock rear suspension that, yes, would become a feature of top-end motorbikes decades later. Moto Guzzi – the company that almost came to own the Vespa brand – got in on the act, too. Its Galletto model was a pioneering and bold mix of motorcycle and scooter – the stability of one, the weather protection of the other – which arguably also demonstrated where motorcycle manufacturers tended to go wrong: a lack of conviction that the pure scooter market was anything more than a rather drawn out fad.

Even the legendary super-bike manufacturer Ducati had a go, and made the same mistake. Its Cruiser – the name says it all against the phut-phut of most models of the era – may have had the world's first electric start for a scooter and its bodywork may have been styled by Ghia, the eminent coach-builders, but its engine was so powerful it had to be

tuned down to meet the road laws of the time. And after that the pricey, super-luxe model was suddenly rather underpowered and ponderous. As time would show, however, it would not be the last attempt at a scooter more Bentley than Beetle.

Now largely forgotten outside of specialist scooter circles – as many of history's best scooters in fact are – there was also Isothermos, or Iso, founded in Bresso by Renzo Rivolta in 1939, just in time to have its fledgling scooter shelved by the events of the Second World War. Had not war broken out, perhaps Iso would have dominated the market and the Vespa and Lambretta never come to pass.

If Iso's aptly named Diva is anything to go by, that could have been the case. Launched in 1957, when the market was certainly mature, it was nevertheless hailed as a new benchmark in scooter design. It had great suspension, easy maintenance and a tubular frame housing a souped-up battery, meaning lots of electrical extras could be fitted – and this at a time when the scooter was increasingly perceived as a luxury item that was more about facilitating your leisure life and looking chic, and a far cry from a basic means of transport that fitted in with bombed-out roads and post-war rationing. It is telling, perhaps,

that Iso was only in production with scooters for another six years, after which it turned its attention to the manufacturing of luxury cars, including the Rivolta, which worked well for a surname perhaps, but, outside of Italy, less well for a product one might aspire to own.

There were other Italian makers, too: Agrati-Garelli, Bianchi, Parilla and Gilera (one of the survivors, its Luciano Marabese-designed Runner proving a hit in the late 1990s). Among them, Aermacchi (like Piaggio originally an aviation company, which built acclaimed fighters for the Italian air force during the war) also fell foul of this misunderstanding of the scooter's purpose. However, perhaps it was on to something, way ahead of its time, when in 1943 and with the war raging, it found the time and materials to construct a prototype electric scooter.

Rumi, founded by Donnino Rumi in Bergamo during the early 1910s as a supplier of machinery to the textiles industry, turned maker of midget submarines, also, like so many Italian heavy industry companies, looked to scooters as a way out of post-war restrictions. Among its stand-out models, the left-field Formichino, or the 'little ant', available, as one ad had it, in 'Paris Grey', was so well, if oddly,

engineered, that its 125cc engine was some 25 per cent faster than comparable machines from other companies, and was said to outpace even most 150cc scooters, such that inevitably it was regarded as the go-to scooter for scooter racers.

But not everything had been thought through for a customer with increasingly high expectations. The Formichino came with a carburetor mounted with a screw that, if tampered with by the owner, invalidated the scooter's warranty; only a Formichino dealer could, month by month, unscrew it bit by bit to open the throttle wider. Perhaps the company did not trust its customers with all that zip. Like so many manufacturers, Rumi, too, quit scooter production in the 1960s, with the market in steep decline, and returned to making unusual devices for the military – for which demand was sadly more predictably reliable.

That decline certainly came hard and fast, so much so that by the mid-1970s the only Italian manufacturer still making scooters was Piaggio. The vehicle much loved but also associated with austerity was unable to keep up with, or propose relevance to the newly affluent. And what they wanted, of course, was a car.

Italy vs THE REST OF THE WORLD

The scooter was by no means an exclusively Italian product, nor was Italy the only innovator in its design, nor did its output dominate sales. Abroad, other makers created some of scootering's more striking scooters. Take, for example, the Mors Speed of 1951, made in France using a cast aluminium frame with cutaway sides exposing the engine; the cartoonish bulbous shape of the Terrot, a 1953 scooter produced by the French motorcycle maker of the same name; the Faka Commodore of 1956, with its jet engine-like air intake under the seating; the Dayton Cycle Company's outlandishly outsized (and aptly named) Dayton Albatross, akin to a sideboard on two wheels; or the fantastical aluminium curves of the 1950s' Maico-Mobil, with its jutting rear end and knight's visor-style apron fitted over a well-sprung space-frame chassis, a package promoted as a 'car on two wheels'

All such models proposed something new for the scooterist, sometimes successfully (at least for a while), sometimes rapidly flopping and disappearing from the market. Intriguingly, national identities seemed to form for each country's scooter manufacturing base, each in pursuit of their own particular, and in hindsight occasionally misguided,

A woman rides her scooter through the New York traffic in **1955**.

The Cushman
Auto-Glide scooter
from 1943.

notion of what a scooter constituted or stood for. Does it speak volumes, for instance, that one of the biggest homegrown hits in Spain – a country which, under Franco's dictatorship, was prohibited from importing scooters (even if it did make Vespas and Lambrettas under licence) – went by the name of the Derbi Masculino, despite its pootling 98cc engine?

Take the Americans, the people who might be justified in claiming the invention of the scooter, if failing to capitalise on it. Prior to the Second World War – in other words, prior to the Vespa or Lambretta – it had an impressive number of scooter manufacturers, from Mustang to Custer, Cushman to Comet, to Bangor Scootmaster and others. But by the end of the war almost none stuck with their manufacture: as Continental Europe would discover a decade or more later, cars seemed the way ahead, especially for those manufacturers facing the biggest consumer boom in American history. Other products just seemed more worth the investment.

Rock-Ola proves a salutary instance. The company was founded in Chicago as a maker of weighing equipment during the 1930s by David Rockola. In 1938 it launched its Rock-Ola Motor Scooter – 'featuring the revolutionary new "Floating Ride"!' –

with the kind of promotional statement that more than hinted at the manufacturer's suspicion that it may all be a bit of a gimmick akin to the hula-hoop or skateboard to come. The Rock-Ola was 'America's Newest Mode of Transportation... Go places, quickly, inexpensively! It's loads of fun to go "scooting"!' Was it any wonder that, at the war's end, it chose to focus on the product for which by then it was already famous: jukeboxes?

Cushman, another manufacturer, offers a cautionary tale. The family business had considerable success with its Auto-Glide models of the 1930s, which probably won it the government contract to devise a folding scooter for US paratroopers during the Second World War. Indeed, much like the makers from the former Axis powers after the war, Cushman's big push into scooter manufacturing was likewise a product of circumstances – in its case the Great Depression. Demand for its Cushman Husky engines, used for power equipment, plummeted. And then more bad luck followed. E. Foster Salsbury contacted the company with a view to buying thousands of the Husky engines to use in his Motor Glide scooter, sending over a copy of his blueprints in the process. But, perhaps after failing to agree on a price, Salsbury decided to use an Evinrude engine instead.

However, Cushman finally decided to run with the idea. The story has it that one Colonel Roscoe Turner, a barnstormer of repute, was an early endorser of the Motor Glide and made an appearance at an airfield near the Cushman factory, using his scooter to get around. A local boy saw the contraption and decided to make his own, using scrap and an old Cushman-made washing machine motor. Over the following weeks he would make many trips to the Cushman factory, where he would buy additional parts, until one day he was spotted by Cushman's boss, Charlie Ammon, and, perhaps more importantly, his 19-year-old son Robert. And it was son who convinced father that making their own scooters would be a good move for the company. After all, motors was what they were good at – and they still had Salsbury's blueprints.

Within a month they had built the prototype of the Cushman Auto-Glide, 'a very crude looking thing', as Robert Ammon would later recall. All the same, its over-confident advertising made much of its technical merits: the Auto-Glide was 'the greatest advance ever made in low-cost motor transportation'; it was

The Cushman Auto King Scooter had a top speed of 50mph and did 100 miles to the gallon.

Teenagers from the Will
Rogers High School in
Tulsa, Oklahoma and their
scooters parked nearby.

'cheaper than shoe leather' and could be run for 'one-tenth the cost of an auto' – or at 120 miles to the gallon. The Husky engine 'whisks you quickly to office, factory, school or a pleasure spin'.

Arguably Cushman's post-war offerings eventually fell victim to the American taste for bigger, faster and more flashy, that saw a scooter as being more a scaled-down motorcycle, than something that met a distinct set of needs. After a series of Italian-style, step-though scooters – the Pacemaker and the RoadKing, for example, each finding it ever harder to compete with actual Italian scooters – came Cushman's Eagle model of 1949, arguably barely a scooter, depending on how strictly one applies Salsbury's criteria. This followed the A-V-8 (as in 'aviate') of 1940, from another maker, Powell, which pursued the same idea of producing motorcycle-type vehicles that, in retrospect, look as though they were made for bikers' children; and also followed the Mustang Colt, which, again, looked more like a toy than anything an adult might ride.

It says much that Cushman faced serious financial problems again when the US government introduced more stringent traffic laws for young riders. And also that, by the time the company wised up to what a

scooter could be – producing its futuristic 720 series – the death knell for the American-made scooter market, indeed, for the scooter market in America, had been sounded. Cushman gave up production in favour of importing Lambrettas and Vespas, but had very little luck selling even those.

Ironically perhaps, one of the only concerted efforts to make what was unmistakably a scooter and not some confused motorcycle-scooter hybrid came from a maker of motorcycles; indeed, the definitive maker of American motorcycles, Harley-Davidson. Unsurprisingly maybe, the so-called Topper, which was Harley-Davidson's only attempt at a scooter – 'tops in beauty and tops in performance', as the ad men put it, wrong on both counts – did not fit well with the company's rough, tough, macho image, quite aside from the scooter's lack of a front brake and rather refrigerator-like unwieldiness next to its streamlined Continental cousins. It did not sell well, not least because by the time it was launched, many scooter operations in the US were winding down. Scooters just weren't hip enough anymore for domestic production.

That the idea of the scooter was not taken all that seriously in America of the 1950s – with its gigantic,

Introduced in 1961, the Harley Topper was the only scooter ever produced by Harley Davidson.

chrome-covered, tail-finned cars, super-sized refrigerators and a general belief that bigger was better – might be suggested by the fact that, if one was so inclined, one might buy one from the Sears, Roebuck and Co. catalogue. Therein one could pick a Cushman, and later a Vespa – rebranded under Sears' Allstate name and dubbed the Cruisaire – and have it delivered direct to your white picket-fenced yard. The Vespa Allstate was only available in green, Vespa being rumoured to have bought up a job lot of army surplus paint for the model. Yet that didn't detract from the Cruisaire's apparent appeal, or its invitation to, as the promotions had it, 'go continental'. In the year it was made available, 1951, the retailer ordered 6,000 Cruisaires. Sears continued to sell a Vespa of some sort or other, eventually just under its own name, with its own blue badge – models that have become highly collectible –until 1966.

Lambretta's earliest inroad into the US market was similarly with an ersatz model, built under licence in Germany by NSU and imported by a New York BMW motorcycle dealership. By 1955 Innocenti had, like Vespa, established its own distribution in the US. Its 'scooter shops' helped make buying a scooter feel

like a great decision in itself, rather than a second best to buying a motorcycle. Not to be outdone by its rival, Innocenti even struck a deal with another major catalogue retailer, Montgomery Wards, to carry its scooters, which it did under the Riverside name. Both catalogues arguably helped the scooter break free of city living by making it easier for those living in the country to order one. The scooter could be just as ideal for quick rural runs as urban commuting.

The US would see another wave of interest in scooters in the 1970s, inspired by the OPEC crisis of 1973, when the Organisation of Oil Producing Countries, less than pleased with America's support for Israel, embargoed oil exports to the West. Suddenly the economy offered by scooters trumped any objections to lack of power or size. Vespa, in particular, capitalised on this, finding a market in the US for models which in Italy were already outdated.

Other nations perhaps fared better in their attempts to get into scooter style. Some much better. Belgium, Holland and France each had their own manufacturers, catering mostly to their domestic markets and rarely seen outside of them. France had such companies as the aforementioned Terrot, as well as Motobecane, with its Moby's

In the oil crisis of the early 1970s, the scooter was an attractively frugal alternative to the gas-guzzling automobile.

American actress Jean Seberg and her French co-star Philippe Forquet on a scooter in Paris in 1962.

distinctive front panel radiator, and even more distinctive lawn mower-style pull-cord starting mechanism – this when the Italians were already trialling electric starters – and Peugeot, among others, many of them with a pioneering background in car manufacturing. Peugeot had made its first motorcycle in the 19th century.

Yet not one, it seemed, of the 12 French manufacturers showing their version of a scooter at the 1954 Paris Motorcycle Show – many encouraged by the French government to do so to stave off Italian imports – were quite French enough to stop national

touchstones of cool, Guy Forquet and Jean Seberg, scootering around Paris on a Piaggio. Gilbert Bécaud, the French singer known as Monsieur 100,000 Volts, even posed in advertisements for Piaggio, claiming 'ça c'est formidable!'.

But it was the British who, while embracing scootering more whole-heartedly over the coming decades than even the Italians (who saw it as a utilitarian and only later as a stylish means of transport), produced scooters with more gusto, albeit far too late in the day to have much impact on the international market. Take, for example, the

handsome Velocette Viceroy, one of a new breed of larger, luxurious scooters, marketed as being 'built for men', as putting those 'days when scooters were just a giggle' well behind its prospective riders. It was new, at least, to Velocette. Its engine was designed in 1957, yet it was not launched until late 1960 and then not available to buy until 1961, by which time its intended customer had already bought elsewhere, or bought a car. In 1958, on the launch of the BSA Sunbeam/Triumph Tigress, its designer Edward Turner – the man behind the classic Triumph Ariel Four Square motorcycle – announced that 'we feel

Left: Potential customers study the latest Lambretta through a shop window in France in the 1950s.

Above: The BSA Sunbeam was also produced as the Triumph Tigress but the differences were entirely cosmetic.

the future of the scooter is assured. We can see the time when the sales of scooters will equal sales of motorcycles.' He was right – only none of them would be British.

Jon Stevens, editor of *Scooter World*, one of the first scooter-dedicated magazines to launch, in 1955, put the problem in much blunter terms: 'People will buy scooters,' he wrote. 'They would buy a British-made scooter if one appeared that would lick all the imported makes. British firms have all the advantages – except brains and foresight and imagination. Scooters are here to stay. They are part of the scene.'

Indeed, many of the new wave of British scooter manufacturers, the likes of Sun, Ariel, Progress, Ambassador and DMW (which, perhaps rather unpromisingly, named its models the Bambi and the Dumbo), as well as scooters from motorcycle manufacturers Triumph and BSA, were being launched just as German manufacturers (see page 62) were closing up shop, feeling that the market had peaked if not already fallen well into decline. Some just hadn't thought things through: the DKW Dove located its large fuel tank in the front body section, dangerously putting all the weight over the front wheel; the Triumph Tigress, by many accounts possibly the best of British scooters, had inspection holes in the side panel for easy maintenance, but these proved so poorly positioned no adult mechanic could use them. It didn't even come with an ignition key – a gift to thieves. Its 1962 follow-up, the Tina (originally named the Fairy, until a wise last-minute change of heart) was riddled with technical problems in keeping with its advertising slogan: 'The scooter that thinks for itself!'.

Yet the signs had never been good, from the British industry's rather inauspicious beginnings. One of the earliest British post-war scooters was the Corgi, said to look like the low and long dog breed of the same name. This was a civilian version of the Excelsior Welbike, devised to be dropped in canisters with British paratroopers to enable both the rapid advance of front-line infantry and provide a means of couriering information when lines might be down. This was in theory at least, if rarely in practice, and all the more so given the unreliability of the engines, especially after having been dropped out of an aircraft.

Made by Brockhouse Engineering from 1947, the Corgi was marketed with probably unintentional

Left: The Triumph Tina was a 100cc scooter designed for short trips.

Below: A Corgi ad from the 1940s clearly aimed at the female customer.

tactlessness as being, as one dealer's ad had it, already 'famous all over the World, with enthusiastic users in more than fifty different countries'. Surely this was not a subtle reference to the many nations in which the Welbike was said to have seen action? Few people in Britain got to ride one: most initial models were sold abroad to help reduce Britain's wartime balance of payments. The Corgi made a show at the 1946 'Britain Can Make It' exhibition in London. Or 'Britain Can't Have It', as the press cuttingly renamed it – most of the products on show were only available abroad. As for the Welbike, in 1946 the British government decided to sell off its dead stock to a New York department store called Gimbels for resale in the US, and this despite a great interest to buy them back in Britain.

While Corgi sales did inspire a few firsts in scootering – their owners took part in the first endurance rides, for example – the scooter looked positively medieval next to a Vespa, even with the 'de luxe' version featuring such tempting advanced technologies as a 'front weather shield' and 'extra-large saddle'. For those who still fancied an airdrop, or who needed to abandon their scooter and jump

Opposite: Mrs
Anita White in
1963 on her
Lambretta
scooter fitted
with a pram
sidecar.

Opposite: Mrs
Anita White in
1963 on her
Lambretta
scooter fitted
with a pram
sidecar.

Right: A young
woman on her
Piattti scooter,
1961.

on the bus, the deluxe version, like its Welbike
ancestor, also folded up. Indeed, although affordable,
the Corgi was, before it was even launched,
effectively superseded by another British scooter,
the Swallow Gadabout, Swallow having been
established in the 1920s as a sidecar-maker by
William Lyons, the man behind Jaguar cars. Swallow
followed the Gadabout with a prototype for a
larger-wheeled scooter called the Joyrider – a name
which would not work well today – akin to the
mopeds the Japanese would have such success with
many decades later. Neither, however, could
compete with the new Vespas or the Lambrettas
just around the corner.

Even a London-based Italian designer could not
necessarily help the fledgling British scooter
industry: Vincenzo Piatti's Piatti scooter, unveiled in
1952 and built by Cyclemaster in Birmingham, was
one of the strangest-looking scooters of the period,
being fat, squat, and with a hovering, height-
adjustable seat of the kind found on a bicycle.
Bicycles influenced other scooter launches, too,
such as that from cycle manufacturer Raleigh, which
made Italian company Bianchi's Orsetto scooter
under licence.

Rise OF THE DEFEATED

Crucially, as the acclaimed motorcycle expert Mick Walker has noted, the British manufacturers simply chose to ignore the growing tide of far superior machines from abroad, while the would-be scooter owner did anything but. Walker quotes one commentator at the 1960 London Show: 'Long famous for powerful motor cycles, [Great Britain] couldn't believe at first that people really wanted these small-wheeled, under-powered models... Fancy, finicky, foreign machines with all the working parts hidden away behind expensive pressings'. Certainly there is some irony in the fact that it was the defeated nations of the Second World War – those that had to reinvent their heavy manufacturing industry – who most fully made a success of designing scooters: Italy, of course, but also Japan and West Germany.

Germany had been slow to take to scooter production, largely due to being been split into western and eastern zones of occupation. But it did not take too long: the 1950 Frankfurt Show heralded its arrival, and by the middle of the decade there were about 20 West German companies making their own scooter designs. And when production did get going it was, wisely, not with scooters to compete with Vespa or Lambretta, or any other nation's offering, but with a whole new class of scooter: the luxury scooter. It was an industry that burned brightly if briefly. Initially, high road taxes and extortionate petrol prices encouraged many of the professional types who would more typically have driven a car to take to two wheels. But these were followed by an economic miracle of post-war reconstruction that encouraged them to abandon scooters almost as quickly. This, in turn, only persuaded the scooter manufacturers to launch ever more upscale models, even if this proved to be largely for export.

The story of Lambretta in West Germany is a case in point. Made under licence for Innocenti by NSU, the German-made models were initially almost identical to those made in Italy. But it was not long before the German regard for over-engineering soon found Innocenti's version inadequate. First NSU proposed making the engine itself, which Innocenti agreed to. But then it was the brakes, the horn, the seats and magneto, not to mention the NSU version adding glove box, ignition switch, speedometer, choke and even a dashboard clock. The copy effectively outclassed the original. When, in 1957, NSU launched its own model, the Prima V, aptly known as the

The Maico Mobil
touring scooter was
often marketed as a
'car on two wheels'.

'Funfstern' or 'Five Star', it was superficially akin to the Lambrettas the company had been making but, in terms of comfort, build and reliability, it was streets ahead. 'Drive better – Drive Prima', as one ad had it.

The Germans were also not blind to the stylistic importance of the scooter. The Prima V came in four colours, even if these were applied with Teutonic exactitude: 'not only sprayed on', as the brochure stressed, '[but] synthetic high-gloss finishes, applied in a scientifically controlled manner and treated by an infra-red process to retain their durable high-gloss finish'. Of course. And yet, three years later, NSU stopped making scooters altogether, switching instead to cars – a move made by many German scooter-makers by the end of the 1950s to avoid financial ruin, and a move ably, if mysteriously, assisted by the West German government's decision to ban scooters from the autobahn.

Cars, after all, were what German scooters really wanted to be, with the one exception of the Junior, a model produced for a few years by the typewriter company Adler, which perhaps suggests just what huge potential the scooter market was regarded as having. But generally, German meant big. You lift the

The Durkopp Diana, a powerful, beautifully engineered 'superscooter'.

bonnet on a car, so why not on a scooter, surmised Puch, whose scooters' bodywork lifted up entirely at the rear to give unprecedented levels of access to the mechanical meisterwerks below. Maico-Mobil, similarly, entered the scooter market in 1951 with what it called – using a line oft-repeated through the story of the scooter – an 'auto on two wheels'. If, despite being a boldly striking, perhaps bizarre design, it clearly wasn't a car per se, then nor, the manufacturer insisted, was it a mere scooter. If other manufacturers had gone to great lengths to stress how scooters were different to motorcycles – some ultimately failing because they didn't appreciate this distinction in the first place – Maico-Mobil was having none of it.

'It is not a scooter,' it declared, 'but a motor cycle with a body giving a high degree of protection against the weather. It is no strain on the rider [of this scooter] to travel 300 miles a day. Such a mode of transportation enables a businessman to retain his neat appearance...'. And to take considerable luggage with him, it might have added. The scooter's huge fairings gave plenty of room for that, a spare wheel, telescopic forks... No wonder King Hussain of Jordan bought one. Maico-Mobil followed in 1955 with its

equally distinctive Maicoletta, all curvy mudguard, retro-futuristic portholes and, despite being a 'scooter', certainly having the performance of a motorbike – indeed, it is considered by some to be the ultimate performance scooter of the post-war era to make it into production. It turned heads, or at least those fast enough to keep up.

Performance was a selling point for the revealingly named Tourist too ('no hill too steep, no road too rough, nowhere too far', as one ad boasted). It was made by Heinkel, a company established in 1922 and manufacturer of some of the Luftwaffe's most effective bomber aircraft during the Second World War and, like Piaggio, making the most of that aeronautics expertise and the best of being banned from aircraft production after the war. The Tourist, one of the first production scooters with an electric start, was seen as much on the race track as on the road, often competing well against motorbikes and having the distinction of taking first place in its class in Britain's first ever scooter race, at Crystal Palace, London, in 1960 – a blow perhaps for those locals who still bore a grudge over the war.

The Durkopp Diana proved an even greater slap: trumping anything the British could make, and the

Italians to boot, this model was prized for its combination of engineering excellence and stylistic flair. Zundapp, another German maker, cheekily drove that point home, calling its most significant model the Bella, Italian for 'beautiful'. It is a name greatly favoured over that of rival Austrian scooter manufacturer Lohner, with its 1957 model, the Sissy.

Japan, too, its economy devastated by the War, would enter the scooter market with gusto. It has come to be better known as a manufacturer of mopeds, beloved by pizza delivery companies the world over – this thanks to 1958's Honda Super Cub proving to be the best-selling powered two-wheeled vehicle of all time, with over 30 million of them sold, despite the boxy plastic body that had seen it and the competitors it inspired dubbed 'Tupperware' models in the US.

But Japan also offered a less well-known selection of scooters, which would dominate the domestic market, squeezing out even Vespa and Lambretta. The manufacturers best known now for motorbikes and cars – Honda, Fuji and Mitsubishi – all produced scooters. Mitsubishi, wartime makers of the Zero fighter plane, effectively produced a straight copy of the Lambretta LC, right down to small details of styling. BSA Sunbeam and Triumph were among other

manufacturers who faced the same problem of plagiarism, yet none ever took legal action. Similarly, Mitsubishi's more successful Pigeon model borrowed heavily from the American Motor Glide scooter.

Yet while copying was at the time something of a bad habit for Japanese industry – as it would become for that in China – this is not to say Japan's scooters were all without originality. In fact, Fuji's Rabbit, as roughhewn as its design was, was launched in 1946, the same year the first Vespas rolled off the production line, although only eight Rabbits appeared off Fuji's line that year. Rapid mechanical improvement and a greater individuality in styling, which, mimicking American post-war design perhaps, favoured a lot of chrome trim, soon saw Fuji models cut a more distinctively individualistic dash. Honda, already established as a world-class manufacturer of good-value motorcycles and motorcycle engines, seemed to launch its own scooter simply because its rivals Fuji and Mitsubishi had done so. It launched its first Juno in 1954, by which time there were 500,000 scooters being ridden in Japan. It was a handsome design with long, slicked-back lines, and the last of its variants – the acclaimed M85 – was launched just 10 years later, when the company nevertheless decided to

Top: The Mitsubishi Pigeon scooter dating from 1949.

Centre: The Fuji Rabbit, produced in Japan from 1946–1968.

Below: The Honda Super Cub – in production since 1958.

return its concentration to motorbikes. And, of course, making as many Cubs as it could to keep up with demand.

The fact is that even for giant, well-resourced, technically experienced companies, the scooter business was a precarious one, tricky to make headway in and deadly for those who got the design or engineering wrong. Chasing the Germans, British motorcycle manufacturer BSA, for instance, launched its own, promising 200cc Beeza luxury scooter in 1955. But its performance was so lacking from the outset it never went into full production. Indeed, trying to make a scooter something that it could barely convincingly be – refined, well-appointed, notably comfortable, genuinely car-like – was something Piaggio and Innocenti had the good sense never to attempt, preferring rather to emphasise simplicity and practicality.

Such was the initial success of their models that by the same mid-1950s period, when British, German and Japanese makers were already on their way to winding down their scooter-making operations, only minor changes had been introduced to the Italians' aging designs, each a refinement rather than an overhaul. That just didn't seem to be necessary.

Scooter style

FROM HOLLYWOOD TO MOD

Previous page:
Mods and their
scooters on the
seafront at
Hastings in 1964.

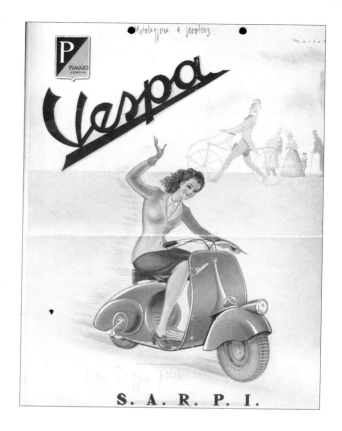

The motorcycle may long have embodied a certain way of life, its iconography of the open road implying not just freedom from societal constraints but a certain outsider, a rebel status. The clothing – all that black leather – is highly suggestive: of dark forces, fetishism, power. And then there is the machismo and adrenaline of speed. None of these qualities could be attributed to the scooter. But if it didn't suggest a way of life, from its post-war re-imagining onwards it certainly suggested a certain lifestyle.

Indeed, this was something Piaggio in particular recognised at the outset. It was at pains to stress how its scooter was not a poor man's alternative to a motorcycle, but rather a new breed of transport altogether, best for convenience over short, typically urban distances. (That said, it was not above playing that card when it worked: an early 1960s ad for the GS150 – or 'Vespone', the big wasp, for many the finest incarnation of all Vespas – dubbed it, 'the scooter for the man who wants power, speed and performance with safety [offering] that exhilarating feeling, surging forward at a touch of the throttle... Perfected for the sportsman.')

As noted, the step-through frame, which, visually, ensured the scooter could not be confused with a motorbike either, made it equally appealing to women as to men. Some scooters perhaps played on this fact a little too much, even for more paternalistic times: one period ad, for the Triumph Automatic, made great play of having 'two controls only – a twist-grip accelerator and brakes'. 'Now you can all get about', the main caption read, over an illustration of a man holding a lady's handbag and gingerly gesticulating that she take the controls. Somehow, she looks terrified. This was despite the fact that, time and again, advertising and other promotional material for various scooter makes would feature a woman at the helm. Even if she was, inexplicably,

Left: A Vespa ad from the 1940s emphasises the fun aspects of the machine.

Below: Lambretta focused on leisure and everyday pursuits in its scooter ads.

often wearing a bikini or short skirt, these ads were designed to appeal to emancipated women, not to catch the wondering eye of those men who might be lured away from their leathers and grease. 'Independence. The girl that gets ahead gets there on a Vespa', as a British ad of 1961 had it.

Wisely, Vespa decided – or, less kindly, following the collapse of its deal-making with Moto Guzzi, was forced – to control the entire marketing of the Vespa. One early masterstroke was to sell them only through Lancia showrooms – Lancia widely regarded at the time as being an upmarket car marque. In the UK they went one better in building the association between scooter and a certain classiness. Imported models of the 125cc Vespa were first seen in the London showrooms of H.A. Fox and Co. Their usual product? Rolls Royce cars, no less.

Over the decades the message in advertising would on occasion, depending on the market, revert to the practicality of the scooter. One exemplary ad for the US, from 1964, ran under the clever headline 'Maybe your second car shouldn't be a car', and went on to neatly summarise a scooter's appeal, and confront typical objections: 'Don't laugh,' it began, 'It makes a lot more sense to hop onto a Vespa than it does to climb into a 4000lb automobile to go half a mile for a 4oz pack of cigarettes.'

Summarizing the engineering genius of the design, it noted how a Vespa has only three moving parts – 'there's not much that can break'; that monocoque

Left: A Lambretta advertisement highlighting the detail of the scooter's technology.

Below: Glamour was also a recurring theme in scooter advertising. This dates from the 1940s.

construction – 'it's not bolted together. It can't rattle apart'; and even turned what some regarded as a lack of hard American manliness into a positive – 'The Vespa is a motorscooter, not to a motorcycle. There is no social stigma attached to driving one'. It concluded with what Europeans already knew. 'You may laugh at the Vespa today. But tomorrow when you're stuck in traffic and one scoots by, remember this. The laugh is one you.' Other ads would veer towards the esoteric: 'Whoever Vespas, eats the apple' is a caption that possibly makes more sense to Italians.

But the general thrust was based on the appeal of the scooter as lifestyle accessory, as modernistically cool, as of the zeitgeist in the way few motorcycles could be. Piaggio best drove home the idea of its scooter being a sexy, chic product, but an affordable one – a mass-consumption vehicle of convenience, sold like any other consumer good, but with a forward-looking lifestyle sheen. It even created a coveted annual calendar – akin to Pirelli's famed tyre version – featuring a number of scantily clad young women in various poses along with their favourite two-wheeled runabout.

But it was product placement that became the key way of underpinning this idea, notably in the movies.

Eddie Albert, Gregory Peck and Audrey Hepburn pose on a scooter for publicity photos for the film *Roman Holiday*.

Stars such as Marilyn Monroe, Sophia Loren, Anthony Quail and, somewhat conspicuously, John Wayne, were among the Hollywood greats snapped on their scooters, which often provided a convenient way to cover the sometimes considerable distances between studio lots. One unlikely publicity image shows Charlton Heston pottering along on his Vespa in full 'Ben Hur' garb. Lambretta was able to corner the services of a visually appealing Jayne Mansfield, who sat astride one of the company's scooters pushing bullet bra forward as if proposing an alternative scheme for streamlining. Debbie Reynolds and Grace Kelly both got onboard with Lambretta, too, while Ursula Andress and a bikini-clad Racquel Welsh posed for Vespa. Henry Fonda was snapped getting off his Vespa GS, wearing suit, overcoat and hat; Jack Hawkins, star of classic British war films, rode a Vespa, which the company capitalised on; racing driver Stirling Moss swapped his usual grease-and-speed environment for a Vespa 150 New Line, which he was photographed proudly taking delivery of; even British comedians Eric Morecambe and Ernie Wise posed at the Douglas Vespa works on scooters being prepared for the 1964 Veteran Vespa Rally.

By then most Vespas on the road were barely 15 years old, but that was considered sufficiently veteran – indeed, the very first Vespa rally was believed to have been organised by sports journalist Renato Tassinari, later the founder of the Vespa Club of Europe, who put out a call for Vespa riders to gather at the annual Milan Fair in 1949, not expecting over 2,000 to turn up.

Most famously, perhaps, Audrey Hepburn and Gregory Peck astride a Vespa in Roman Holiday (1953) – in which the hero convinces a traffic cop to let them go because they are 'going to church to get married on a scooter' – only further served to associate the scooter, and, more specifically, Piaggio's scooter, with all things stylishly Italian. And especially Italian in the flouting of any safety regulations; on several of the different promotional posters for the movie, Peck is seen riding his Vespa with Hepburn perched on the handlebars and a photographer riding backwards on the luggage rack.

Vespa was leader among scooter manufacturers to make good use of the 'win-a-scooter' competition, too. Vespa gave away a Sportique model to a teenager as part of a cinema chain competition to promote the release of *Summer Holiday* in 1963, the

Right: Movie
legend Paul
Newman travelled
around Israel on a
scooter in the
early 1960s.

Opposite: Italian
boys pose with a
scooter in
Sambiase in
southern Italy
during the 1970s.

scooter being presented by its star, Cliff Richard. In an earlier tie-in, in 1959, rising star Patricia Karim rode the new French-made 125 ACMA Vespa in the French film *The Heat of Summer* and promoted it in the accompanying poster campaign – a promotion that worked: when the film was released in London, some 600 members of the Vespa Club parked up outside the Tottenham Court Road cinema, bringing traffic to a standstill, and reporters flocking to the scene.

If a film prominently featured a Vespa, as in *No, My Darling Daughter* (1961), Piaggio or a local dealer would be quick to provide one for a newspaper competition. Promotions were not above utilising a pretty smile and a pair of long legs: the Miss Vespa Darling competition became a long-running tradition at Vespa clubs, the winners even meeting at national finals, one of whom, Anne Turner, winner of the 1966 competition, was presented with a 90 Model scooter by future James Bond, actor Roger Moore.

Such associations helped define the scooter – and the Vespa in particular – as much as a lifestyle choice as a means of transport. This was clearly something many manufacturers pressed home at any opportunity, perhaps especially within the trade,

hoping that local dealers would see potential in the same pitch. Douglas Vespa, for example, gained a reputation for the innovativeness of its motorcycle show stands: in 1952 it devised one that appeared to show a Vespa balanced atop a fountain of water; in 1960 it showed off the latest model atop a giant revolving glass jewel.

The launches would become more spectacular still: forward to 1979 and journalists were being taken to Monte Carlo's chichi Sporting Club to the unveiling of Vespa's new Si model, which was delivered suspended under a helicopter.

Of course, while other nations' manufacturers arguably produced better scooters than the Italians

To continue to appeal to a stylish market, launches for both Lambretta and Vespa, grew ever more elaborate.

– more powerful, more well-appointed, just as innovative and distinctive – it was at least in part the very Italian nature of the Vespa and Lambretta alike that drove their appeal at a time when, post-war reconstruction notwithstanding, Italy was coming to be internationally recognised as the global hub of pioneering design and fashion, a reputation that was still on the up well into the 1980s. The exoticism that Italy suggested was captured in one instructional ad, for Vespa's Ciao moped, as late as 1968: 'Spell it Ciao. Say it Chow. Ride it Now.'

The Italian heritage of the scooter was certainly a large part of its appeal to a group that would, in the UK and later the US at least, come to define the scooter as a style icon: the Mods. Certainly Lambretta pursued the development of its brand name with gusto, with considerable advertising, as well as much publicity seeking via its backing of various (often crazy) record attempts. That, in 1997, long after Lambretta had ceased production, the Lambretta name still had sufficient cachet to be applied to a British, Mod-inspired men's clothing line (the name used under licence from its Italian owners) perhaps spoke volumes.

WE ARE
the mods

When *Quadrophenia* was released in 1979 (a film of The Who's concept album) Mod became a mainstream fashion phenomenon. High-street fashion brands launched Mod lines, Mod iconography – the RAF roundel, the Union Jack – was plastered over anything that would sell, while the music industry attempted to launch Mod bands. However, going mainstream signalled the death of Mod for anyone who was, or had been, a purist of what might be called a style philosophy.

Mod, after all, was a London scene predicated on difference, on one-upmanship and individualism, on being an outsider. And because there was no one uniform, it was hard for the press to identify Mods as a tribe, which allowed them to stay underground for longer. But, as a culture, it could not survive its tenets becoming merely part of everyday fashion, indeed, shaping everyday fashion for the next generation.

While several revivals have heralded a new wave, the first, defining era of Mod occurred in the early 1960s, when mostly male dressers turned away from the UK and towards the Continent, Italy notably, and American Ivy League style for their smart fashion cues: in direct contrast to the mostly teen Teddy Boys before, who had looked to the past for

Mods with their scooters festooned with multiple headlamps gather outside the labour exchange in Peckham, south London in 1964.

ASHLEY LENTON
the Vespisto

As Coco Chanel put it, fashion fades, but style is forever. And that is just as well for Ashley Lenton. 'I bought my first scooter in 1968 when I was 16, just when they were going out of fashion', says the scooter historian and editor of the magazine of the Veteran Vespa Club, based in the UK. 'The Mod phenomenon was dying, even if scooters hung around afterwards. In fact, you couldn't get rid of them, so you ended up just keeping the one you had. And in my case that was until the end of the 1970s, when in the UK there was the mod revival. For the best part of a decade my friends and I had London all to ourselves for scootering.'

Not that, for Lenton, the scooter was ever about personal transport – as important as that aspect was to the success of and appeal of the scooter more internationally. While he concedes that Vespa was more his preference through circumstance than through careful deliberation – 'the reality is that at 16 you buy the same as whatever your mates have got, even if in later years you find more technical reasons to justify what was an emotional choice,' he jokes – he did indeed come to love the style. 'To justify my choice of Vespa accordingly I would say that its appeal was as a piece of design: the early Vespas, which didn't change much, were pure form follows function, a real aesthetic pleasure. The Vespa was stylistically perfect to me.'

It is an appreciation that has not waned with the years. After all, the club of which he has been a pivotal member for some decades concerns itself only with geared models. Perhaps the more surprising aspect of it, however, is that for many of the several hundred dedicated members, the interest in things technical stops there – with the gearing. Lenton says that most see the Vespa not simply as a design icon, but as exemplary of arguably the most iconic in visual and popular culture of the 20th century.

'There is,' as the 1964 Vespa GS and 1977 Vespa P200 rider puts it, 'a never ending demand for 1950s and 1960s style – but very definitely an end in demand for 1950s and 1960s mechanics. That is what has driven the 21st-century demand for replicas and re-builds that put modern engines into old scooter bodies, and which has even informed the scooter designs coming out of Piaggio. It is the vintage look that matters.'

Certainly, some take that appreciation to extremes, preferring their scooter less in pristine form, so much as showing all the bashes and bruises of its long life. Lenton describes it as being akin to the long lasting, late 20th-century fashion for vintage items in clothing and interiors, in which 'the wear and tear represents not just a lost heritage but a certain authenticity – an authenticity in the flesh, so to speak. I have seen that affect the price of a scooter. In fact, unless you are going to do a full and expensive restoration, and not just a 'blow over' or a quick re-spray, then you are best leaving it alone. There is even debate as to whether it is best to treat any rust or let it be, because rust is all part of the vintage look. Mods may have preferred their scooters pristine, but to have a scooter in the 21st century that was actually part of mod history, the chances are that it will definitely be showing signs of age.'

Clearly the aesthetic considerations for the vintage or veteran scooter fan run deep. Clearly too, there is a nostalgia to it all. Lenton says that members agree that there was a simplicity to the early scooter style that has been lost over the years, much as the mechanics have grown more complicated too. 'Back then you could fix things yourself, but with a modern-day scooter that is getting harder and harder for an amateur to do,' he says. 'That is perhaps a reflection of society at large, that many things have lost a certain simplicity of character, even if they have become more efficient or reliable. But something is lost too. Whereas, for example, it used to be a real thrill to ride your scooter from London down to Brighton [about 60 miles], and a sense of achievement in making it, to a modern scooter that is nothing.'

And perhaps that sense of a bygone age – 'the golden age of scootering, at a time when convenience and technology were in balance with a personal freedom of which the scooter was just part', as Lenton puts it – will in time pass completely. The Veteran Vespa Club, like many clubs of its kind, does what it can to act as conservator of scooter history, but similarly finds that often museums and institutions are reluctant to hold the finest examples of veteran scooters for preservation or will do so without guarantee they will not sell them eventually. And, meanwhile, interest in veteran scooters is fading with each new generation, and each new fad.

'Future generations may look at granddad's eight or 10 scooters and maybe want one – as a piece of furniture. Or may keep another, but want to put in a modern engine. Future generations may always want to ride what looks like a vintage scooter, but they will want what is mechanically new,' argues Lenton. 'That means that in time there will be just a handful of genuinely vintage examples in garages and museums and the rest will be scrapped. What interest there will be in them will be in their style.'

Indeed, could it be the scooter's good fortune to have been created in an era for which there is a seemingly enduring appeal and fascination, especially for those not even alive at the time? Might that prove the vintage scooter's saving grace? Maybe. 'Vespa, Lambretta, the Mini Cooper, the Jaguar E-Type – these vehicles have such strong associations with the style of the 1960s period, associations that will always be there and always find fresh appeal, whereas the Wolseley Car Club [the marque having had its heyday pre-Second World War], for example, is probably not going to do so well because it won't be able to attract new people.

'The fact is that 60s style is hard to better and will always reignite new passions,' Lenton adds. 'The vintage scooter isn't just a representation of a certain aesthetic, however great it is – it's also a representation of a certain time and place. It's part of the package, with the music, the clothes, the attitude. With vintage scooters the cultural aspect is always in play.'

Right: Mods and their scooters outside Soho's Scene club in 1964.

Opposite: A Lambretta customised with multiple mirrors and headlamps.

inspiration, Mods, as their name suggests, sought only all things modern. It was the first fashion based on the pursuit of the new. Not short back and sides but a college boy cut. Tailoring wasn't drape, like the Teds, but single-breasted, narrow-lapelled, fitted, vented; ties narrow, too; trousers slim; shoes chisel-toed. Tennis shirts, boating blazers, desert boots, Harrington jackets and shrink-to-fit Levi's jeans – much of it sold on a black market by American GIs still stationed in the UK – were all part of a more casual Mod look.

Mod was constantly seeking this week's look. Influential Mods – 'Ace Faces' – set different styles, albeit with twists unnoticed by the uninitiated. Women also adopted Mod style; in fact Mod introduced the idea of some clothing as unisex. More importantly, it helped make both an obsessive and individualistic approach to clothes, and conservative dressing – particularly distinctive from one's forebears – socially acceptable. Mod defined youth dressing.

That, at the time, was defined as expensive and hard to come by – much was bought on the new system of hire purchase, and much had to be made-to-measure, which saw the working class sons

of London's East End Jewish tailoring trade lead the way. Coffee bars, and later live music venues, became hubs where styles would be shown off – and where modern jazz would be listened to, or American R&B, soul, whatever music was new – with customised (i.e. 'individualised') Italian bicycles and later scooters proving the ideal form of transport between these increasingly disparate venues. Parkas – in easy supply thanks to post-war US Army surplus – became a convenient means of protecting one's precious and carefully curated clothing while on the move.

Their scooters may have been chosen in part for their Italian flair, in part because they offered that independence and ease of travel between the various

cultural hotspots around town, but they also became part of the image. Some Mods chose to accessorise their scooters with as many lights, mirrors, protective chrome and other trinkets as possible – with bonnet mascots liberated from Jaguar and Mercedes cars one option – or, at least, in the popular imagination they did; such excessive accessorizing, in so-called 'Christmas tree' fashion, was not actually as widespread as might be believed.

This is not to say that scooter manufacturers, and other companies, did not see great potential in the sale of accessories to Mods and other enthusiastic scooterists. One figure, quoted in the 1957 *Scooter Year Book* says that, 'for every £1 spent on scooters, you can estimate that 2 shillings [10 per cent more] will be spent on accessories', half on functional additions and half on comfort and aesthetic touches. Windscreens were especially popular – by the late 1950s some four out of five scooters had them fitted by owners – as were luggage carriers. Rear panniers were popular, despite making a rear-heavy machine even more imbalanced, with some making do with a tartan carry-case fitted behind the leg shield. Designer Max Rhiando even invented the Scootokaddy, a glass fibre box, which fitted over the

front wheel's mudguard. More fancy additions could include toe protectors, port holes, wheel trims, spot lamps and flag masts – these last two being Mod choices in particular.

Those Mods who did load up on additions favoured the more powerful scooter models – a Lambretta TV or SX, or a Vespa GS – since a large engine was required to carry the considerable extra weight. Lambretta always found the UK to be its biggest foreign market: in the Mod mind, the modern world was streamlined and deserved a streamlined scooter, the likes of Lambretta's TV175 Slimline of 1962 perhaps, or 1963's TV/GT200, the fastest Lambretta available at the time, offered in five colours, and produced specifically at the request of Innocenti's British importer. Modish Liverpudlian band Gerry and the Pacemakers even managed to get a special-edition Lambretta model named after them: the Pacemaker.

Often finances trumped desire; many Mods, after all, were barely out of school. The Lambretta Series II TV, a model made up until 1963, was, for example, a popular option because of its more approachable pricing. Indeed, some future Mods first brush with the sub-culture was seeing older boys riding their

A group of mods on the seafront at Clacton in Essex in April 1964. The town was one of a number of places where Mods clashed violently with their rivals, the Rockers, who wore leather and rode motorcycles rather than scooters.

scooters to school – typically in defiance of the rules – and parking them up just outside the grounds.

Inevitably perhaps, the sheer popularity of scootering as linked to the Mod sub-culture – part of fashion whether it liked it or not – condemned it to going out of fashion, and by the late 1960s, with a

new, long-haired, hippy-inspired, psychedelic agenda shaping youth markets, Mods were on their way out, scooters too perhaps. Between 1959 and 1973 the scooter market in the UK shrank by some 75 per cent, with similar collapses in sales seen across Europe. 'Get flower power with your new psychedelic

Phil Daniels as Jimmy Cooper in *Quadrophenia*, the 1979 British film film which fictionalised the mod culture of the early 1960s.

Vespa, available only from hippy Eddy Grimstead', as one key British scooter dealer of the period put it in a hopeful advertisement of the time.

Some might argue that Mod tarnished the scooter; after all, Mods, together with Rockers, comprised the original folk devil, a concept introduced by sociologist Stanley Cohen in 1972. The folk devil was the subject of a media-fuelled moral panic, blamed for rising crime, bouts of personal violence, perceived as an organised threat to society's moral norms. Certainly the well-publicised clashes between the Mods and Rockers, which turned quaint British seaside towns such as Margate and Clacton into places to avoid in 1964, did not help the scooter's cause. Others might note that a wealthier populace simply preferred a car – youths too, given the chance, and especially given its advantages in courting young ladies. And yet...

The importance of *Quadrophenia* as a cultural catalyst in the scooter's revival cannot be underplayed. While the original Mod scene had effectively passed into history – with the exception of a few diehards – the movie introduced its precepts of dressing and scooter style to a new generation, albeit in a way that, to original Mods, could verge on

pastiche. Its effect was keenly felt in the UK: fired by a new wave of enthusiasm for scooters, the Lambretta Club of Great Britain threw a members-only event over the August bank holiday of 1979 and effectively re-booted the rally calendar.

By 1984 the Isle of Wight rally was able to attract a staggering 12,000 people. Come 1986 and such numbers were out of control, with the Isle of Wight rally witnessing riots and looting that reignited the reputation of scooterists as a public menace – precisely the reputation that the scene had been trying to move on from since Mods and Rockers clashed in those (subsequently much media-hyped) seafront battles during the early 1960s.

But *Quadrophenia* also resonated as much in the US, for example, as it did in the film's home country. It focused new interest in scooters for ska and punk fans, especially among people of college age, and encouraged the adoption of other established British sub-cultures such as rude boy and skinhead, as well as those still in the making such as the psychobilly-inflected scooter boy and – a much more US-specific phenomenon – the mechanically-minded scooter girl, with the scooter girl's ride of choice, the Vespa Primavera 125.

CHAPTER 3

LET'S GO

CLUBBING

Let's go racing

All together NOW

All hobbyists tend to coalesce in clubs eventually; it is a way of sharing one's perhaps particular passion with people who understand it, rather than find it strange or trivial. And the scooter was no exception. Such was the ease with which the scooter became an integrated part of so many owners' lives (the very appropriate use of the word 'owner', as opposed to 'rider', which seems reserved for motorcyclists, speaking volumes) that they quickly became objects around which groups of the like-minded wanted to meet. Early scooterists had even got into the habit of saluting to each other when passing, acknowledging the particularity of their preferred mode of transport.

The sheer rapidity with which the club scene had taken off was a phenomenon in its own right. Take, for example, the Vespa Club of Great Britain, one of the first and what would become one of the biggest of European scooter clubs. It grew out of the more local North-West London Vespa Club, the first in the UK, formed in 1952 by a railway engineer who had recently bought one of the Douglas-made Vespas. Within seven years the UK alone played host to some 120 scooter clubs nationally. The following year the London branch held an event at the city's Harringay Stadium with sufficient interest that the Vespa Club

of Great Britain's initials – or at least three of them, 'VCB' – could be spelled out in the massed ranks of several hundred scooters parked on the pitch.

By then, every western European country – Norway excluded, the weather seemingly to have precluded interest in scooters there – had a national Vespa club, overseen by the Vespa Club of Europe. Such clubs would provide a means of keeping on the road, through the sourcing of replacement parts, for example, long after even major manufacturers such as Lambretta had ceased to operate.

Much as the scooter might be considered the motorbike's quirky cousin, so, too, were the club activities associated with it. Posing outside the famed Ace Café, near London's A1 road, with one's Triumph or BSA was perfect for the leather-clad machismo of the motorbike's clan. But for scooterists, at least initially, something much more genteel was called for. What in retrospect might seem like quaint gymkhana-style events (derived from competition between mounted British soldiers serving in Raj India) were typical at rallies: one could expect to see the skills required of scooterists to tackle the fearsome water splash, or the challenging see-saw obstacle, much as, in years to come, rallies in the US would run

a slow race, the winner being the last scooter to cross the finishing line.

How about formation riding? About 15 scooterists, dressed in white overalls and helmets, hanging on to two Vespas in various poses – for which a British team took home the trophy from a European-wide gathering of Vespa fans in 1957. Or, the following year, the British Vespa scooterists again winning first place in the national dress competition, for which they had paraded on two wheels complete with bowler hats, pinstripe suits and furled umbrellas. Other events included long-distance riding – the petrol company Esso sponsored a 'Scoot to Scotland'

NICK ROBINS

the club man

Nick Robins had made his mind up about scooters from a young age. 'I was exposed to classic scooters even then, through my uncle, who had P-range Vespas, which at the time not only seemed quite cool, but also represented freedom. I just fell in love with these toy-like, somehow bizarre two-wheelers that you just pointed in the right direction and off they went. Even as a boy a scooter felt attainable to me – even though my uncle kept warning me how much trouble they were. I was growing up in Australia, too, where my real interest in classic scooters was further ignited by the 1990s Britpop scene, which made it over there from the UK. The scooter suddenly seemed like the nucleus of a much bigger scene. Everyone else I knew was into racing cars with V8 engines – so I also knew I must have been weird.'

Unusual in Australia perhaps, but having moved to the UK, Robins was soon able to parlay his newfound passion into ownership of a series of vintage models, each in his care for little more than two years at a time, and each reflecting a period in his life. He started out with a 1979 Vespa Primavera ET3, 'which was a bit comical, seeing as I'm over six feet tall, so looked like a gorilla on a tricycle. But I was riding the fastest hunk of junk in London and that scooter re-captured all my youthful dreams of scooting.' He followed that with a metallic green 1967 Vespa GTR, on which he experienced his first crash: 'driving into the bar of a car – the driver of that was not best pleased', Robins notes, and onto which he 'bolted so much chrome that I couldn't weave between the traffic anymore'. Then he

moved up into the big league, commissioning the building of a 1964 150cc Vespa VLB, with 10-inch tyres – in part as a result of successfully persuading his then employer to lend him the money. That was followed by a Vespa GS – 'the ultimate London mod scooter', Robins suggests, a 1966 Lambretta Li150 and a 1963 Lambretta TV175.

Come 2004, however, and Robins, who works in museum management, would make his passion for scooters most official by joining, and later running, one of London's most famed scooter clubs, the Bar Italia Scooter Club. The name speaks volumes about the club's approach, being borrowed – with its approval – from London Soho's listed landmark café. The club – one of central London's very few scooter clubs, despite the city embracing the scooter to beat the congestion – was founded only in 2002, despite Bar Italia having been a meeting point for Mods and their scooters, as well as other scene-makers through the decades, since the advent of café culture in the UK of the 1950s. The café opened in 1949 by Lou and Caterina Polledri, initially as a hub for the immigrant Italian community in the area. Parts of its initial red and white Formica table and bar tops are still in use, and the Gaggia coffee machine has been there for over 50 years.

'Scooters are in part about a way of life from a particular time and Bar Italia is part of that,' says Robins. 'It gives the club a certain vibe – it's synonymous with Soho – but also a responsibility, there's brand to maintain, if you like'. Indeed, in part because of its

association with the historic Mod haunt, the club is often requested to work on Mod/scooter-related projects, from a launch for Fred Perry, to presenting Olympic cyclist and Mod fanatic Bradley Wiggins with a scooter, to providing and managing the scooters used on the shoot for the movie re-make of Brighton Rock (2010).

'The club is not like any other scooter club I've visited,' adds Robins, 'in that we're a Mod club, but Mod in the strict sense of always trying to look for whatever is new and fresh. We're not the pig-headed type of club that insists you must only like music released between 1958 and 1964, or whenever. We just take a modern outlook.'

Not that the Bar Italia Scooter Club is entirely without focus. 'We're a mix of people who ride scooters, some just because they're a great means of transport and make the commute to work easy, others who are very much dedicated to a scooter lifestyle – they're into their ska music or the Casuals [a British football and clothing-based style sub-culture of the 1980s],' says Robins. 'But the common denominator is the machines – the aesthetic, the engine, the pose.' And so the Bar Italia Scooter Club only admits those who ride geared scooters. 'Automatic scooters represent progress in many respects, even if they are more examples of function over form,' says Robins. 'But we're about preserving the aesthetic of geared scooters, which is sheer bloody-mindedness on our part really. No one has ever really challenged me on why we have that rule. We just do. Beyond that, however, it's all camaraderie.'

Top left: A
competition to
find the most
attractive couple.

Top right: Women
compete in a
scooter race in
Milan, 1952.

Below left: A
more challenging
race through hilly
terrain.

Below right:
Andre Baldet
scaling Mount
Snowden.

ride from London to Edinburgh, for instance, an event which by the mid-1960s was attracting 400 scooterists –as well as many more left-field trips that aimed to test the durability of scooters and perhaps the sanity of their scooterists with ever stranger record attempts.

There was, for example, the endurance ride. In 1950 Lambretta took what had already been established as a 12-hour duration record when three scooterists shared the task of riding a Series B model 989 miles at an average speed of over 82mph. The Isle of Man, host to the famed TT motorcycle racing event, held a scooter alternative incorporating several different trials, a hill climb and sand racing. Speed, too, meant there were records to break. In 1951 Romulo Ferri took his stripped back and streamlined, super-charged 125cc Lambretta and achieved just shy of 125mph from a flying start, a record which (for the engine size) stood for more than 20 years.

Equally ridiculous – at least to the motorcycling fraternity – was scooter racing. This had developed with the creation of the first sports scooters, around 1955, but soon led to a number of international events for the various classes of scooter: 24-hour endurance racing, Le Mans for scooters, became something of a fad, with standard scooters typically used, and some adapted with racing carburettors or extra large aluminium fuel tanks to minimize the need to stop.

Then there was the wacky ride. In 1957 Jeff Parker and friend Lewis More rode two new Model D Lambrettas the 340 miles from Edinburgh to Fort William in Scotland. However, this wasn't what made it wacky; rather this was to break the scooters' engines in ready for the 4,406 feet ascent of Ben Nevis, the highest peak in Scotland. Only Parker made it: it took him five hours; More dropping out after suffering clutch problems, almost halfway up the mountain. In 1955, Snowdon, the highest peak in Wales, was also climbed by Andre Baldet riding his 125cc Vespa fitted with sandbags of ballast to prevent it tipping back on the steep incline.

Of course, manufacturers tended to support such feats whole-heartedly, in part for the publicity, in part because they demonstrated the positive qualities of their little machines. In 1959 Tommy Behan and Joan Short, members of the Vespa Club of Great Britain, rode their GS Vespa from London to Paris on just £1 of petrol – not a small sum then, but demonstrating

Romolo Ferri made many attempts at world land speed records for Lambretta during the 1950s, sometimes in a fully enclosed version of the scooter.

remarkable economy all the same. In America, one scooterist covered 30,000 miles in six months on a round-the-nation ride. But occasionally these feats also crossed the line into the purely absurd. Piaggio's enthusiasm for backing record-breaking attempts, for example, saw it assist George Monneret to ride a 125cc Vespa from Calais in France to Dover in England – yes, the scooter was mounted on floats and powered by a propeller attached to the rear wheel. It was a trip he made in six hours on his second attempt, the first having been thwarted by a piece of driftwood, which damaged his paddle; on arriving in England the floats were detached and, James Bond-like, Monneret rode on to a celebration event in London.

Much as clubs in those nations that embraced the scooter were about celebrating it, elsewhere they were a means of keeping interest alive in a market in which the scooter was all but dead. In the US, for example, and even after major brands like Vespa had closed their dealerships during the 1980s, an alternative market quickly appeared. Small scooter workshops specialising in restoration, repair, supply of parts from old inventory or via import, such as First Kick Scooters in San Francisco, Vespa

Supershop in San Diego, Scooters Originali in New Jersey, became recognised and respected names on the US scooter scene. It was through such businesses that scooter riders were able to keep their machines on the road, which in turn allowed clubs to proliferate.

The more modern rally was another animal. Just a snapshot of the national scooter clubs operating in the US, for example, in the early 2000s would have included the likes of San Diego's Secret Society, founded in 1983, creators of Scooter Rage, one of the nation's largest scooter rallies; the Secret Servix, established in Denver in the late 1990s, North America's largest all-female scooter club, which runs an annual 'Friday shopping ride', with each member carrying a purse of silk-screened ribbons which they award to anyone they consider stylish; through to Michigan's Jedi Knights, established in the late 1990s and the country's largest scooter club, with chapters subsequently opening in many cities including New York, San Francisco and Denver – its motto being, appropriately, 'world domination', its members having to be knighted with a light sabre. And if the idea of chapters makes these clubs sound akin to notorious biker gangs like the Hell's Angels, that is not entirely

IAN GRAINGER

scooter boy

Mod may have been a seminal moment in the British style culture of scooters, a stereotype the media has done much to underpin – indeed, in the public imagination, scooter riders are, by default, Mods. 'But that started to become ridiculous, not least because it was inaccurate,' says Ian Grainger, scooter aficionado and author of Scooter Lifestyle. 'By 1983 or so, following the Quadrophenia revival, you would start to see 50 or 60-year-olds at scooter rallies dressed up as Mods. And they would get called 'comedy mods' – even if they had been real mods 20 years earlier. But a lot of people were starting just to get tired of being labelled as Mods when they clearly weren't, or when Mod suggested something dated on the British scooter scene.'

The answer was, as Grainger was to find, to define oneself as was dubbed – without any great imagination admittedly – a 'scooter boy', a breed most typically found in the Midlands, north and north-west of England (a product, Grainger theorizes, of the favouring of scooters as a youthful means of transport between disparate and poorly connected pit villages).

'The scooter boy almost defined themselves in opposition to everything Mod,' he says. 'Mods were always into looking good, of course. They had the pristine clothes, the good haircuts, the carefully looked-after scooters. Scooter boy was almost a protest against that. We wore old army clothes, Dr. Marten's boots, denim

jackets covered with rally patches, sometimes with the sleeves cut off and worn over a nylon flying jacket. It was much more practical. I wore a Barbour jacket and a helmet. You were more interested in being protected than looking a certain way, not in wearing a parka that would be soaked through while on a 200-mile ride to a rally.'

Not that the clothing choice was always practical: it could make you a marked man. 'You could go to a rally and you could always spot anyone into scooters, even if just walking around the town, by the way they were dressed,' says Grainger. 'That helped give a sense of belonging. But it also meant that scooter boys would find some places wouldn't let them in. You would see signs outside saying "No Scooter Boys", like the old sign "No Coloureds, No Irish, No Dogs". You would never get away with that now.'

It was, in fact, in part this social ostracism that would later encourage some scooter boys, Grainger among them, to 'feel the need to dress up a bit'. The scooter boy would become, as Grainger calls him, 'the scooterist'. The scooterist's consequent style of choice – 'Levi's jeans, Clark's boots, T-shirt and jacket, with some favouring technical jackets by makers the likes of Stone Island' – would lean towards that of Casual: the seminal if largely unsung British men's style tribe of the mid-1970s to mid-1980s, ground-breaking in its introduction of sportswear to everyday fashion. In the search for working-class sartorial one-upmanship, exotic new

foreign sportswear labels were sought out – the very labels that had become newly accessible to young football fans now travelling abroad to watch their teams' away matches. Much like the Mods before, with their emphasis on the new and on constant change, so Casuals would turn the terraces into a weekly catwalk of their latest selections.

Every sport was examined for the possibilities of its boldest, brashest, most colourful and graphic clothing – none of them characteristics that could be applied to standard menswear at the time, but suitable, one might imagine, for the similarly bold inventiveness of the period's British scooter scene. This would lead to a rediscovery of long-established and long-forgotten old mannish brands such as Farah, Burberry, Aquascutum, and pioneering an international interest in mostly Italian designer labels such as Armani, Cerruti and Valentino. How the clothes were styled was as much part of it: wide-wale cords, for example, might be split at the seam so they sat better over one's rare Adidas trainers, or cut and not hemmed to create a fringe of loose threads; shirts would be worn buttoned to the neck. Mod, and scooterist, ran through the attention to detail.

But all that was to come. Grainger recalls that while scooter boy style was essentially laissez-faire – 'almost punky', he says – in part because of the scooter boy regard for psychobilly bands (The

Meteors and King Kurt), 'with a touch of skinhead, in fact there were a lot of scooter skins' – it was a laissez-faire approach that was applied as much to the scooters. 'It was less about embellishing scooters as Mods did as stripping them down to the basics. You had skeleton scooters – so you'd take all the panelling off a Lambretta to reveal the engine – and those on which the apron was cut away. It was a big thing to paint your scooter matt black or army green, which I never did, or to tune up the engine and give your scooter race colours. It looked rough and ready, but was actually quite considered. You might have a nice paint-job, but it would be metal flake and nothing retro.'

Unsurprisingly, says Grainger, who himself still rides a race-tuned Vespa PX200, as well as a 'slower but more reliable' Vespa GTS250, there was always a lot of friendly rivalry with the Mods: 'Lots of name calling, lots of taking the mickey'. Equally unsurprisingly, it made the scooter rallies of the 1980s visual spectacles: 'To be able to ride for hundreds of miles, take over a town and see hundreds of scooters and their riders from all over the country was very exciting,' he says. And especially for a man so impassioned by the machines that he formed a scooter club while he was still at school, organizing the hiring of a coach to take him and 40 friends to their first scooter rally. 'Of course, there were those people who went to rallies who did so just to show off their

scooter. They'd take it there on a trailer, which was another thing scooter boys mocked. For us scooter boys it was all about the ride, and, even more than that, the socialising.'

That rally scene may have consequently suffered its peaks and troughs. To better control attendance, and police trouble, the National Runs Committee – a now defunct body that organised the major national rally calendar – required the carrying of ID cards, 'and that put a lot of people off,' says Grainger, 'since it seemed to go against the spirit and spontaneity of the events and of scooter riding.' But, he notes, much as old Mods never die, the original scooter boys of the 1980s have never gone away. Many – having taken a break to start families, for example – have returned to a vibrant rally scene revived by a younger generation discovering the scooter, and by even yet another Mod revival, albeit that perhaps they are now more inclined to attend regional events closer to home than to scoot long distance for a damp weekend away in a tent.

'In fact, now you get some 50 or 60-year-olds at events and they're dressed as scooter boys again,' he laughs. 'That says something about how important the lifestyle was for them. I don't think anybody has come up with a mocking name for them just yet, but I'm sure there will be one in time.'

inaccurate: Denver's ACE club, founded in 1990, operates under the unforgiving motto 'cocaine, scooters and whores' and espouses a hedonistic lifestyle – and a smart line in slogan T-shirts ('Lots of Bottles, no Rockets', reads one) mostly being jibes at other Denver scooter clubs.

Meanwhile, the rally scene of the 1980s and early 90s could be just as boisterous. In the UK it might feature performances by scooter-style bands, such as The Meteors and King Kurt – of the psychobilly school popular with scooterists – or Bad Manners – of the ska-inflected party-pleasing school, equally popular – or, in some instances, Oi! bands – right-wing leaning and, inevitably, bringing with them an additional, unwanted, often troublesome element, not least street fights along (superficially at least) left/right political lines. Custom scooter competitions aside, the rallies also appreciated other curves via the likes of wet T-shirt contests.

This was much rougher and readier but also much less straight-faced than the Mod stereotype of scootering suggests. Indeed, the rat bikes and DIY custom builds had their own, decidedly un-Modish style: side panels were removed and engine parts polished, the leg shield cut away with an angle grinder, motorcycle fuel tanks fitted and the bodywork painted matt black, through to the more artistic and expensive chroming, engraving, spray-gun work or metal-flake paint jobs, the cables covered in multicoloured wrap.

Opposite: Twenty-first century scooter fans at a rally in Southend in 2007.

Left: Skinheads tended to view their scooters as transport rather than a statement of style.

descendant of Mod, even if it was culturally different. But much as Mod gave way to Skinhead, so it also gave way to the Scooter Boy, then in his late teens or early twenties. Scootering was a genuinely youth phenomenon, and an inclusive one too, a shared passion for scooters being enough to unite people of diverse tastes and backgrounds.

Inevitably perhaps, as the rioting and burning at the Isle of Wight scooter rally of 1986 best, or worst, exemplified – with the following year seeing a Sea Scouts boat set alight at the Rhyl rally in Wales – rallies could spark trouble, entailing heavy policing. The Margate rally – Margate being the site of some of the famed clashes between Mods and Rockers two decades previously – even had its own mobile police station. Police would instigate on-the-spot searches of scooterists and their scooters, looking for offensive weapons and checking vehicles and their documentation were 'in order'. The use of CS gas to break up crowds was not unknown, and certainly local authorities reacted with the same extreme caution, and unqualified lack of welcome, to any scooter weekender taking place on their patch.

Local stores might hire security staff and supermarkets would remove alcohol from their

The riders also developed their own general change in style: out went Mod affectations, in came more practical attire the likes of army surplus combat pants (the latter-day equivalent of the Mod parka perhaps, also worn in part because army surplus was plentiful), T-shirts, rally patch-covered sleeveless denim jackets and nylon flight jackets, primarily the MA-1 – standard issue service kit for USAF fighter pilots since 1950. Indeed, many of the elements of scooter boy style had a crossover with that of another British style tribe of the period: skinheads and scooter boys alike favoured the MA-1, bleached jeans, polished oxblood-coloured Dr. Martens boots, even the flat-top and closely cropped skinhead haircuts. Skinhead had been a direct

A collection of rally patches on the back of a jacket showcases a huge range of styles.

shelves. 'Scooter Scum' became the media's new folk devil. 'Invasion! Barriers go up at Smallbrook Stadium', as one newspaper headline of the time put it, documenting how the area's water supply had been cut off and toilets removed, just to make sure that attendance was especially unappealing. Sometimes scooterists had to worry about their scooters or parts being stolen. Some events set up protected areas in which one's scooter could be left safely while the festivities went on.

Such developments might well be considered teething pains: in time that troublesome element was weeded out, or lost interest, and rally organisers upped the ante to run their events with more professionalism. In the early 1990s, BritPop, like Quadrophenia before it, sparked a mainstreaming of scootering. This may have frustrated the diehards, for whom the fraternity of scootering now seemed to be co-opted by pop stars and endless promotional campaigns alike, but it also changed the public's attitude to scootering and scooterists. Not only were rallies now welcomed as annual cash cows for local economies, but a new generation of retro-inspired, twist-and-go scooters seemed ready to introduce two wheels to a new rider.

Nor was the scooter scene of the late 20th century merely a British or American affair, even if the considerations of style and the more tribal nature of scootering belonged more distinctly to their cultures. Certainly, for every nation that had caught the scooter bug, there was a scooter clan. Only the Italians, of course, did it smarter. There, in the spiritual home of the scooter, the early 1980s saw a sandwich bar become an unexpectedly inspiring place for a youth sub-culture to begin – Al Paninos, in the Via Agnello district of Milan. The culture was subsequently christened Paninaro by the *La Stampa* newspaper, its followers Paninari. And, like their British equivalent, Casuals – at the time more concerned with kicking off at football matches than kick-starting scooters, but whose dress choices would later become a default style for older scooterists – for them it was about the expression of wealth and status through clothing. But, crucially, their own carefully curated selection of clothing.

Indeed, the flashiness of the *Paninaro* – embodied in teens and young twenty-something men – was in some sense a statement against the drabness of much Italian urban life through the 1950s, 60s and 70s, but also of aloofness from the political strife and

Stylish scooter fans were among hundreds of riders at the Bar Italia Kickstart Rideout in 2012.

uncertainty that also engulfed the nation over these decades: notably the battle between right wing and communistic political extremes and the threat of terrorism. The Paninari certainly underscored their own vision of shallow, cosmopolitan living – *la dolce vita* for beginners – through their fashion choices, which tended to lean towards the colourful and luxurious, worn in an almost stereotyped Italian way: sweaters draped over the shoulders, trousers or denim cut or rolled short to the ankle, no socks, puffa jackets. But they also reflected a certain (apolitical, consumerist) nationalism.

While Americana was a key part of the look – such brands as Timberland deck shoes, Vans, Schott leather jackets and Ray-Ban sunglasses – more favoured were less well-known homegrown brands such as Fiorucci, Moncler, Controvento, Best Company, Stone Island and CP Company, as well as young designer brands, the likes of Armani and Versace. Transport from sandwich bar to sandwich bar – notably branches of the now defunct Burghy Milanese fast-food chain, which were their secondary hang-outs – was, inevitably, by Vespa, although the large-wheeled scooters like the Scarabeo appealed to their Mod-like desire to be of the moment. The devotion to scootering was one reason why Paninari also favoured boldly coloured back-packs.

Distinctively for a sub-culture, the Paninari made no attempt to keep the movement underground, self-consciously detached from the mainstream or out of public view. Rather, they embraced media attention: throughout the 1980s, several magazines including *Paninaro*, *Wild Boys* and *Preppy* were published documenting the Paninaro culture and its scootering lifestyle, with, in 1986, the Pet Shop Boys' song 'Paninaro' bringing it more international attention. So well known were the Paninari in Italy that TV comedy shows even lampooned their look.

PADDY SMITH
the rally patch king

A field in Skegness, a dour seaside town in the UK, may be an unlikely place to start a minor cultural phenomenon, but then Paddy Smith's was an unusual business: that of rally commemorator and merchant of memorabilia. The art school graduate grew up with scooters. He was given an Excelsior Monarch for his 16th birthday, 'a rare and valuable scooter now, but then it was the most uncool thing on the planet,' Smith notes, leading him to swiftly sell it and buy a Vespa Sportique. But come the late 1970s his affair with two wheels was long over.

Until 1981, that is, when his brother-in-law, and his Lambretta Li150, persuaded Smith to come along to Skegness, at that time one of the major spots on the British scooter rally calendar. Not one to miss a sales opportunity, Smith designed and printed 15 T-shirts to take along to sell. 'Whilst these flew out as soon as we reached the pub, everyone was asking if I could make patches too,' Smith recalls. 'I noticed that a lot of people had parkas and flight jackets decorated with these cloth patches [another trick would be to sew a bar towel onto the forearm of a flight jacket, specifically to use to wipe your scooter seat down after rain], so I promised to be there with some at the next rally, in Yarmouth.' Again, he somewhat underestimated demand: he printed 50 – 'a very crude, one-colour print on grey cloth,' he says – which quickly sold out. That day he earned more than a week's wages, and a business was born: 'We did five more rallies that year. I remember staying in a B&B in Brighton and laying on the bed throwing pound notes in the air. And

I guess it was after that success that my wife Annie convinced me to quit my job and go it alone.'

What Smith cannot have appreciated at the time was the deeper significance that his designs would achieve – such that his name became a generic term for any cloth patch bought to commemorate one's attendance at a particular rally. Rallyists would be sure to make a point of buying their 'Paddy Smith' on the first day, rather than risk them selling out. Worse than not getting your patch was wearing one of an event one had not actually attended. This was frowned upon within the British rally-going scooter community.

'Everyone had a sense of achievement at reaching their rally destination on their scooters and resented that 'plastics' [as those half-heartedly devoted to the scooter scene were dubbed] were sporting medals they had not earned,' as Smith puts it. 'That original principle changed by the late 1980s when people would ask their friends to bring them one back if they missed a rally, but it was generally accepted that these would not be sewn on. A lot of people bought two patches – one for the jacket, and one for the collection. And they wanted a full set for that.' Those with spares might swap or trade more classic designs. 'Older patches pass hands for quite surprising prices now,' Smith notes.

'Most of the patches I printed at that time were based on sketches supplied by clubs, which I tidied up a bit and printed in one or two colours as either 6-inch square or circular designs,' says

Smith. 'Rally patches featured line drawings of standard scooters or, in some cases, no scooter at all; for example, as with the pop art-inspired 'See you next year folks' patch designed for the last rally of the year, held in Colwyn Bay.'

But Smith was also aware that, covetable as his designs were, he could not command a monopoly: a growing number of rally patches were sold in the pubs, albeit often just on a small scale to fund the individual's rally weekend. Smith boosted the desirability of his by creating a rarity: while other patch-makers off-loaded their excess inventory in shops in London's Carnaby Street, Smith pledged that his patches would only be available at the rally they were made for. He made sure each design was copyrighted, notably after they began to attract black market copyists. He formalised the style and format of his patches, so they were 'instantly recognisable as what became known as a Paddy' he says. He even settled on patches being roughly 4-inches square; at that time there were nine official scooter rallies in the UK and nine patches sewn together neatly in a block fitted perfectly on the back of a denim or flight jacket, which by the 1980s were popular choices on the post-Mod British scooter scene. Later Smith even designed his patches as collections, so that a set of all nine would work in unison to reveal a bigger design (he gave prizes for the first person to collect all nine and identify this design).

But, perhaps above all, he invested in reprographic equipment and greatly improved the look of the patches, making them a class above more amateurish options. Whereas previously he might draw

a generic scooter for his latest patch, he began to use actual, identifiable, rally-going scooters as his models. Each patch came signed by Smith, and featured a logo spelling out 'scooter rally' and, later, just 'run'. '1989 to 1992 was probably my most creative period,' Smith says, and one of his busiest, as his patches were now being produced for rallies in Germany, France, Holland and Belgium.

'Continental scooterists adopted many of the styles created by the British scene, where the Mod, Mod revival and scooter boy cults had originated. This included the wearing of patches, and this continues today, even though Germany and France in particular have evolved their own styles of scooter customization and dress,' Smith adds. 'By the mid-1990s the scene in the UK was waning too, such that patches were becoming less of an obsession and those who continued scootering or started to do so were adopting more practical and protective clothing to ride their scooters.'

By then Smith had rediscovered less oil-stained artistic pursuits, moving to France, where he opened a gallery. He continued to make patches for clubs in the UK, Australia and across Europe, to revive some of his best designs as 'Paddy Smith Originals' and to fight the imitations widely available on line, or at least ensuring that they were billed as 'not Paddy Smiths'. After all, if you weren't there, don't wear the patch. Not that Smith's love of scooters diminished as it once had – far from it. For his 60th birthday Smith and his two sons rode to Naples. 'We were actually heading for Tunisia,' he admits. 'But we broke down too many times.'

ON YOUR *marks*

While style was a chief appeal of the scooter to many of those who bought one, their functionality could not be ignored, and many attempts were made from the Second World War onwards to find other utilitarian uses for the little two-wheeled machine. Various police forces around the world were quick to order their own scooter variants, some slightly souped-up – most were used for traffic control, so the power to catch up with speeding offenders was required – others fitted with two-way radios and special paint jobs. As one piece of promotional material produced by Douglas Vespa for the UK market dryly noted, a police scooter would 'aid the efficient running of any local authority'. Or perhaps, a tourist board. Through 1970 the oil giant Texaco ran what it called its 'Tourist Pilot' programme in cities across Norway, Sweden and the UK: attractive women dressed in sky-blue uniforms scooting about on Vespa Super 150s ready to provide free assistance to any tourist who needed directions or information about the locality.

Sidecars also had their moment, in an attempt to make the scooter a viable form of transport for tradesmen: the Vespa Commercial, for example, was a box sidecar capable of carrying 125 pounds. Fears

that this would make the scooter unappealingly slow were tackled by some dealers demonstrating that, even with sidecar attached, the rig was still capable of pulling a trailer with another scooter mounted on it – the whole set-up being driven around town to help spread the word. Other tradespeople saw similar potential for a promotional opportunity: in the UK, a bakery company, Procea, had its sidecar recreated as a giant loaf of bread, thus serving as novelty ad and delivery vehicle in one. Vespa, of course, produced its own three-wheeled scooter-come-truck, the Ape, which experienced varying degrees of success in different markets. In many it seemed just as practical to just use a mini van, with four wheels – the Ape seemed a step too far away from the scooter's original genius intention.

Next to a motorcycle, a scooter perhaps seems an unlikely candidate for racing. And yet, as well as the many distance records that the major manufacturers attempted in the early post-war decades, speed also certainly had its draw. Take, for example, the motor racing star Romolo Ferri, who on one day in 1951 achieved acclaim, at least among scooterists, by cracking five world scooter speed records, including covering a flying start kilometre in

17.95 seconds. That meant he powered his heavily adapted Lambretta along the Munich-Ingolstadt autobahn all the way up to 125mph. This topped the 100mph-plus speed record previously held by, of course, Lambretta's arch rival Vespa. The company's works tester, Snr Mazzoncini, took his one-off Vespa Streamliner to those speeds along the Rome-Ostria autostrada and, as the company took pains to later note, did so without the super-charger used in the Lambretta run.

Racing had perhaps been encouraged by the evermore powerful run of scooters launched by both Piaggio and Innocenti through the late 1950s and early 60s. The Vespa GS150, for example, launched in 1955, put paid to the idea of the scooter as under-powered, under-appointed and merely utilitarian; its follow-ups, the GS160, SS180 and Rally 200 saw engine sizes creep up and up. Innocenti's Turismo Veloce had such power that, of course, better braking was required. The model was the first production two-wheeled vehicle with a front disc brake, a feature that did not become standard on many scooters until the 1990s. And more power always seemed like an option. After all, around 1950–51 Innocenti went out of its way to prove its manufacturing credentials in

this area by producing a 250cc v-twin grand prix motor racing cycle, designed by Pier Luigi Torre, and said to be a warning to the Italian motorcycle manufacturers to stay clear of scooters or expect the makers of Lambretta to respond in kind by entering the motorcycle market in full force.

PAUL ROBINSON
the fanatic

Paul Robinson knew that he wanted one the first time he saw it, back in 1999. 'I'd never ridden scooters before and had no real interest in them,' says the journalist and photographer. 'But this really stood out. It looked like nothing else on the road. And then there was the performance, of course, which appealed at a time when I was going through a boy racer phase. The advertising of the time said, "It goes like the proverbial" [from an English expression ending "shit off a shovel", suggesting great speed]. And that said it all to me.'

The scooter was the Italjet Dragster, launched in 1998 and dead by 2003, when Italjet faced financial difficulties and finally went bust. Such was Robinson's immediate devotion to this scooter – with its Ducati-inspired bodywork and exotic fork-less front suspension – that he bought one of the first batch to be imported to his native UK, and within a few months had launched a website and forum (which he has since sold) devoted to the adulation of the Dragster. He had no idea that this passion was shared.

'But before I knew it there were 100 members, then 200 a few days later, then it snowballed,' he says. 'The Dragster was loved because it was so futuristic, a scooter for a new era; it was history in the making, not poring over old Lambrettas. There was nothing nostalgic about the Dragster. Italjet was bold in taking a radical design, said to have literally been sketched on a napkin, and actually making it. They were ahead of their time. I think it even appealed to those who more typically attended classic scooter rallies, which perhaps were starting to feel a little stale. Dragster riders wanted to get noticed.'

Indeed, Robinson was soon exploring an international, if somewhat underground appreciation for this then radical looking machine – he found himself in Sweden, for example, where he discovered a group of 'Dragsterati' who liked nothing more than to partake in illegal drag racing over eighth-of-a-mile runs around industrial estates in the dead of night – and from that Robinson launched his own X-Race series back home, although his were conducted within the law at sites such as York Raceway, Santa Pod and Elvington Race Track. 'You'd find yourself up against riders like jockeys, who obviously had an advantage when it came to the

power/weight ratio,' he recalls. 'They left super-bikes standing at the line. They were crazy times.'

These crazy times were also ones in some sense new for scootering. For one, the Dragster was a celebration of automatic scooters at a time when scooter enthusiasts still tended to revere gearing. It offered all the benefits of an automatic – dependable, accessible, clean, easy to ride – 'but looked cool in a new way too'. Robinson even organiaed one of the UK's first 'ride outs' of automatic scooters from London's Ace Café, the iconic hang-out for 'ton up boys' (Rockers) of the 1950s and 60s, a place which has passed into biking legend. 'Get a lot of Dragsters riding together and it was a great feeling,' he remembers.

And while the British scooter boy culture may have chopped, painted, etched and custom-built some of its most famed scooters, the Dragster scene was, as Robinson calls it, 'totally reductionist – customising with the Dragster was all about stripping away, not building up. This scooter for the 'Max Power' generation was about less adornment, not more, in a way that made it the very opposite of the Mod mentality.'

Robinson might not have been able to resist a custom paint-job: his 'Freak' Dragster had a grey-and-white camouflage inspired by a Norwegian warship. But strip he did: mirrors were removed, so too the Dragster's mobile phone compartment, and the pillion passenger seat; the number plate bracket was shortened. Some changes were more aesthetic: concealing the Dragster's battery under the seat to better reveal the scooter's trellis frame; others were all about weight: the standard exhaust was replaced with one much lighter, as were the mudguards and steel floorboard, even the tax disc holder. Anything that could be changed for a carbon fibre alternative was replaced.

And that was not the only tinkering, of course: tuning to give the Dragster speed to match its reductionist looks was also a popular, if often illegal activity in the UK, providing way too much horsepower – perhaps 36bhp, instead of the factory standard of around 11.5bhp – for anyone without a full motorcycle license. Riders would sometimes mount cameras on their Dragsters to record their burns and stunts.

'That sort of horsepower was a huge leap and, combined with a much lighter machine, basically meant you had to learn how to ride it again,' says Robinson. 'You had to ride with your body weight shifted forward in order to keep the front wheel down because otherwise it would lift so easily. Sometimes, of course, you'd let it go up and show off with a wheelie. But I had a few scary incidents and decided to stop that. There was an immaturity to it all, of course. But there was definitely a movement going on, a movement inspired by a single model, which is amazing.'

One, certainly, that Robinson misses. 'Sometimes that era feels like yesterday, even if now there are other guys doing other custom work with other models of scooter,' he says. 'But once you have had a Dragster, you always remain an enthusiast.'

Rider Don Moya
takes a corner at
higher speed than
his Lambretta with
painful results.

While scooter clubs had boomed throughout this period, their focus tended to be chiefly social. But with increasing power under the fairings, a sportier side grew increasingly popular. By 1958, the first World Scooter Rally – the result of a smart tie-up between the National Scooter Association and the tourist board of the Isle of Man, in the UK – was being held alongside the famed Tourist Trophy (TT) motorcycle racing event (just how indicative this is of the imagination of the tourist board at the time is hard to say, but the cover picture of the free souvenir programme for the 'Isle of Man Motor Scooter Rally, 1962' fails to include any scooters at all).

Even established TT stars, such as Freddie Frith and Denis Parkinson, took part on machines much smaller than they were used to, although, unlike the TT races, the 12- and 24-hour scooter tests were conducted on open roads and within the speed limits. The event was positioned as something that would elevate scootering to a new seriousness. If the 1957 Isle of Man event – an unofficial dry run – included such competitions as the 'Loving Cup', for best scooterist couple, the organizers of the 1958 event promised that it would not cater 'for the spit-and-polish boys with Simoniz polish on the brain and a

curvy girlfriend (non riding of course) on hand to enter the 'Miss...' contest.'

The need for speed soon caught on. Come 1960 and the British mainland saw its first scooter race, staged at the Crystal Palace circuit in south London – it comprised six laps of the 1.14-mile circuit. However, style was hard to leave behind. One trade paper, Motor Cycle, noted that many of the scooters had their 'panelling and weather shielding looking more ready for a concours d'elegance than a road race'. The same year – encouraged by this new vogue for competing on scooters – saw the first attempt to define what a scooter actually was: according to the Federation Internationale Motocycliste, a scooter was (among other criteria) a two-wheeled vehicle on which a rider could sit without being astride a frame; had a minimum of 25 centimetres space forward of the seat; a rim diameter for both wheels of not more than 16 inches; had a kick-starter or other starting device; and a leg shield or similar apron of more than 40 centimetres in width. Suddenly scooters that thought they were scooters – the German Maico-Mobil, for example – were no longer, even if they still were not the cars on two wheels they promised to be.

It was, perhaps, a renewed emphasis on technology over style that encouraged a revival of scooter racing in the 1990s (much as BritPop was reinvigorating interest in the scooter as a style item at the same time). Throughout the decade racetracks up and down the UK – Cadwell Park in Lincolnshire, Pembrey in Wales and Snetterton in Norfolk – would regularly be busy with scooter race meetings. Several classes of race existed, but among the more hotly contested were the so-called 'standards', which saw Lambrettas and Vespas, with engines around the 150cc or 200cc capacity, go head to head.

For the more aggressive rider, there were the 'specials', in which scooters tended to be specially tuned and physically adapted for racing. The latter would include the stripping away of any extraneous weight, which might even include removing the fuel tank, the fuel instead being carried inside the tubular steel frame, and the addition of certain motorcycle parts, from fairings to seating, that provided a more aerodynamic edge. Tuning would provide perhaps 250cc of power.

It was in these makeshift attempts to provide a better racing machine that many of the high-specification characteristics of later scooters – from water-cooling to fuel-injection and disc brakes front and rear – were first experimented with. Arguably they would also inspire a healthy business in kits – from manufacturers such as Polini, Imola and, perhaps most famously, TS1 – that allowed road-going scooter enthusiasts to modify their engines to enhance performance. Later a category designed specifically for 70cc automatic scooters would be introduced, a category that came to be dominated by the Piaggio Zip, given its impressive weight to power ratio and, as the name suggests, its sheer 'zippiness'.

It was also at this time that the demand for sport models really began to create a new scooter category in its own right: machines often priced akin to motorcycles, with the aforementioned advanced spec to boot. With them went a new kind of styling – nothing retro, nothing Mod, but the brash paintwork and decals of professional racing motorbikes. Formula One proved a direct inspiration to one of the first models launched in this class: racing crews used their own hyper-tuned, beefed-up scooters to move around the pits in a situation in which time-saving was crucial. And inevitably it was a Formula One team that inspired the first commercial spin-off of this ethos: the Williams Italjet Formula 50

was a hi-tech model in its engineering as much as in its styling – check out the twin exhaust as it burns away into the distance.

It soon encouraged the launch of similar speedsters: the Malaguti F12 Phantom – scooter or fighter jet? – the Honda X8-R, Piaggio Typhoon, Derbi Predator and Peugeot Speedflight. Those working in the naming departments of the respective manufacturers clearly had the expression of testosterone in mind. Italjet created arguably the most impressive looking of the racing scooters, its Dragster – with a mere 49cc engine but that striking Ducati-inspired trellis frame – and Formula models. The 125 and 180 variants featured very high-performance two-stroke engines, of such performance that typically they did not meet national road safety regulations.

It was in this segment of the scooter market that mechanical technology – considered by the riders to be as important as the look, if not more so – was pioneered. Aprilia's SR50, introduced in 2001 as the answer to Italjet's models, not only had a liquid-cooled engine, but its later update had the manufacturer's 'Di-Tech' or direct injection engine, making it one of the greenest and most economical – not to mention speedy – scooters available at the time.

It was in this part of the market that a new scooterist was born: concerned less with history, retro style, rallies or custom artwork, but with speed, speed and more speed. The archetypal boy racer of souped-up cars was reborn on a scooter – a Gilera Runner perhaps – powering around estates, pulling wheelies, helmet characteristically worn perched to the back of the head – within the law but only just.

PETER BURLEY
the trial rider

'I had a dabble with grass racing, which on little wheels was interesting,' recalls Peter Burley. 'In fact, I came across my old leathers the other week. They don't fit anymore unfortunately. I tried hill climbs, too, which was a question of either a timed straight run up quite a steep hill – to say the least – or on zigzagged tarmac, in which case it was a question of first to the top. Some races were all over in 30 seconds.'

Burley has tried most means of competing on a scooter in his time; indeed, it was what you could do on a scooter, rather than too much obsession with the style, badge or club affiliations that seems to have appealed to him most. But it was the loneliness of the long-distance scooterist that really caught his imagination: trial-riding's demand of covering hundreds of miles over a pre-arranged route and in a specific time frame, checking in at various control points along the way.

'It is,' he says, 'more a test of navigation and of endurance. You may only have to average 25mph over the distance, but when you factor in that that may be on country roads, and in the dark, and you have to stop for petrol and at all the control points, you have to get on with it. Lose 45 minutes because you get lost or have to stop for some reason and you're effectively out of the trial. You learn to recharge quickly at the control points, maybe grab a chocolate bar. It's not so easy eating on route with a full-faced helmet.'

It does still grab his imagination. He got his first scooter in 1959 when his father lent him the money to buy an Iso Milano ('the Piaggio factory was striking at the time so no Vespas were available,' he points out), and, many decades later, he is still riding trials that challenge him to travel 540 miles in 20 hours on a 125cc machine. And he is not only riding the trials, he is winning them. 'The average age of trial riders is surprisingly high,' he notes, 'which suggests that it is experience that counts.' And, in some cases, a touch of derring-do. 'I did try night trials through a winter in South Wales once, and it was said that if you could have seen the roads in daylight you wouldn't have done so. The roads were all mountain ash, together with snow and ice. Treacherous really. You had to mount a car battery on the running board to give you extra lighting.'

These days trial riding, although still popular, is perhaps less demanding: scooters are more comfortable, more reliable and, although perhaps not in the spirit of the early trial rides, satellite navigation makes reaching one's next control point considerably easier. Trial riding's golden age, Burley suggests, peaked in the 1960s and was fizzling out by the mid-1970s, a period in which trials regularly attracted several hundred or more riders, and when he might be entering a trial at least every other weekend.

'You would ride all weekend and then straight to work on the Monday – it was mad really,' he notes. 'But the rides gave a real sense of freedom, of escape.' And they often involved some serious journeys, all around the UK, but also to Turin, San Marino, Hamburg, Venice, even Oslo, trials that amounted to 'a couple of thousand miles there and back in some cases'.

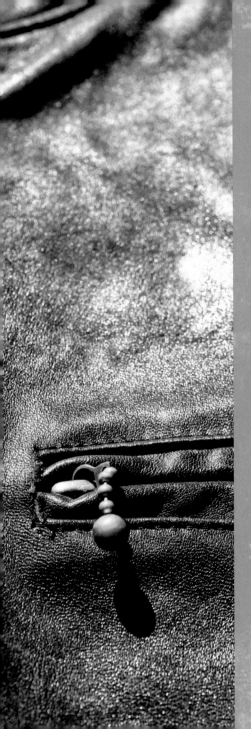

'It was never about how fast you could go; in fact, we often rode against motorcycles with much bigger engines. It wasn't a race and we didn't call them races either – races on public roads are illegal, of course,' Burley notes, with mock seriousness. 'It was about keeping going and knowing where you were going – and working that out was by map, even by the position of the sun. And it was about planning, which was as much fun as the riding.'

Sometimes trials would propose a number of possible routes, so that could mean working out which was the fastest, safest and most efficient (given that riders' mileage was recorded between each control point to prevent cheating). He always wore a good watch. The right clothing was essential, too. Burley chose motorcycle boots, leather trousers and a lightweight scootering jacket with built-in armour – something protective but also comfortable and suitable for all weathers. 'I've done trials in rain so heavy you couldn't see any tail lights ahead, for example; the kind of rain that in any other situation would make you decide to stop. But on trail riding you know you can't afford to stop,' he says.

Typically he would also pack spares – a spare wheel and inner tube, replacement cables. Geared scooters were often favoured even after automatics became available. 'On an automatic scooter, if you get a puncture you have to take it to a workshop and you're out of the trial,' says Burley. That, one senses, would be more than a blow to his competitive spirit. It would simply spoil the journey. 'Of course, getting to each destination along the way was the point of the trial,' he says. 'But more than that what was enjoyable about it was the journey. It was all about the journey.'

Tools OF THE TRADE

Above: Western Union messengers and their delivery scooters, 1940.

Oppposite: A three-wheeled Motorette scooter in city traffic, 1947.

While style was a chief appeal of the scooter to many of those who bought one, their functionality could not be ignored, and many attempts were made from the Second World War onwards to find other utilitarian uses for the little two-wheeled machine. Various police forces around the world were quick to order their own scooter variants, some slightly souped-up – most were used for traffic control, so the power to catch up with speeding offenders was required – others fitted with two-way radios and special paint jobs. As one piece of promotional material produced by Douglas Vespa for the UK market dryly noted, a police scooter would 'aid the efficient running of any local authority'. Or perhaps, a tourist board. Through 1970 the oil giant Texaco ran what it called its 'Tourist Pilot' programme in cities across Norway, Sweden and the UK: attractive women dressed in sky-blue uniforms scooting about on Vespa Super 150s ready to provide free assistance to any tourist who needed directions or information about the locality.

Sidecars also had their moment, in an attempt to make the scooter a viable form of transport for tradesmen: the Vespa Commercial, for example, was a box sidecar capable of carrying 125 pounds. Fears that this would make the scooter unappealingly slow were tackled by some dealers demonstrating that, even with sidecar attached, the rig was still capable of pulling a trailer with another scooter mounted on it – the whole set-up being driven around town to help spread the word. Other tradespeople saw similar potential for a promotional opportunity: in the UK, a bakery company, Procea, had its sidecar recreated as a giant loaf of bread, thus serving as novelty ad and delivery vehicle in one. Vespa, of course, produced its own three-wheeled scooter-come-truck, the Ape, which experienced varying degrees of success in different markets. In many it seemed just as practical to just use a mini van, with four wheels – the Ape seemed a step too far away from the scooter's original genius intention.

CHAPTER 4

Twenty-first century toys

From cool TO CUSTOM

For all that a scooter – a Vespa or Lambretta in particular – might represent design classic, needing no adulteration, some scooterists have not been able to resist giving them the personal touch. For them, such reverence of a design decades old is to be stuck in the past. Move on, they say: customise. The factions of scooter customisation are certainly diverse. There is still the world of the historically accurate restoration, which requires a lucky barn find or paying out for an ever more expensive original 1950s/60s scooter to work on (which made the US a hotbed of restoration, given the large numbers of low mileage scooters available to buy). There are those customisations that demand just a touch of modification, a retrofitted modern engine in a vintage scooter, for example – a more technically demanding job than it may at first seem.

But then there are the rat bikes (as they are more commonly known in the US), the antithesis of the pristine, historically accurate restoration or polished Mod scooter, with its chromed steel crash work aiming at making the scooter yet more impressive, more imposing. These are makeshift, DIY customisations that are more expressions of the owner's random enhancements than any planned project of beautification. The rat bike may be part fibreglass, part chicken wire, part cutaway, with a decoration courtesy of liberally applied house paint.

And, finally, there are the works of art that have come through since the 1980s – painted, engraved, sculpted – for those favouring radical change and the imposition of a more personal design. Here the very structure of the scooter may be altered, cut, chopped and moulded into a new two-wheeled fantasy, perhaps, counter-intuitively, into something akin to a chopper – scooters given often preposterously long forks, or racers – or akin to racing cars, with souped-up engines and decals, ideal for track and (invariably illegal) road racing alike, but perhaps ideal, most of all, for the Concours d'Elegance.

Top left: Artworks of the Beatles adorn a customised wheel guard.

Top right: Corradino d'Ascanio, designer of Innocenti's first scooter.

Below: Custom decorated vintage Vespa and Lambretta scooters.

JOHN SPURGEON
the custom scooter artist

Trained as a graphic designer, working in everything from magazines to set design, it was around 1983 that John Spurgeon noticed a new demand: to decorate scooters. What started as a one-off commission from a local scooter club in Norwich in eastern England, soon snowballed.

'My background was on the art scene, not scooters, although I was always into what was then the underground scene of Northern Soul, which in part had become associated with scooters too,' says Spurgeon, whose company, Aerographics, became the go-to place for high-end scooter art. 'On the one side scooter work was about restoration – painting a scooter so that it looked exactly as it would have done in the 1960s, for example – but then there was the side of the scooter world in which people wanted a certain theme expressed on their scooters – full-blown custom artwork.'

Its subject matter could be wildly diverse, from Bob Marley to The Who, Jesus to Charlie Chaplin to Blackadder (a British hit comedy TV show of the 1980s), through to racing colours and the more heavy-metal-influenced graphics stereotypically associated with motorcycles. 'I've worked on every theme you can think of,' Spurgeon says. 'But if someone goes to the trouble and expense of having custom artwork done on their scooter, often the artwork they choose is very personal to them. It's not following a trend. There wasn't anything that couldn't be done, but certain controversial [far right wing] subjects came up that we wouldn't touch: it was just the rider trying to be provocative.

'And, of course, being different or standing out is good when there is such a competitive element to the artwork, too. Clients want to take their scooters to shows and win,' he adds, noting that such was the intricacy of the work, a single scooter might be four months' work for three artists. 'There's competition between the artists, too, because there are really good artists, and then not so good ones. You always wanted to produce your best work, and you responded to other artists' work you admired, too.

Such was the cultural cachet of the idea that Aerographics soon found itself designing and applying artwork to one-off scooters for promotional corporate use, with brands as different as Donna Karan and Martini, Vivienne Westwood and restaurant chain Yo Sushi all jumping on the trend.

In each case – and at its late 1980s peak, Aerographics had perhaps 25 scooters in for intricate paint jobs at any one time – initial drawings would need to be made to develop the client's idea (this was in the pre-CAD era), from roughs to thumbnails to developed artwork, the scooter then disassembled, each part stripped, then primed, base-coasted and the final artwork applied by hand direct to the panel – a different class to the stick-on vinyl artwork that would come in later.

'At that point it's basically like doing an oil painting,' says Spurgeon, 'but the bodywork of the scooter is your canvas. You just adjust your skills to the surface and size of the canvas. If you're a

good designer, you make it work – and while much has changed about the work, from the use of computers to the quality of the paints, it's the artistic content, and what you can actually do with your spray gun, that counts.'

Like any artist, Spurgeon is particular about his paints and the effects they can achieve: some might have slow-drying properties, for example, which meant they could be moved around on the scooter's metalwork to create a marbling effect, and over which translucent coloured paints could then be applied. Since, he says, most clients would still want to continue to ride their scooters – even if just to the rallies where they would compete – the upper layers of lacquer used would also have to protect the artwork below, to guard against petrol, salt and UV damage, as well as the elements. 'The scooters had their accidents, of course, but they were rarely deliberately damaged,' says Spurgeon. 'There was too much respect for them and the work.'

'The paint itself had its own fashions, too,' Spurgeon adds. 'There was a trend for translucent paints with gold leaf, for example. In fact, the whole move to put artwork on a scooter has moved in and out of fashion. Thirty years after doing a job on a scooter and you suddenly see it around on the scooter scene again. People get it out of the garage and decide now is a good time to show off their piece of art.'

New models
FOR NEW SCOOTERISTS

Perhaps the most crucial new launch in Vespa's revival during the 1990s was the four-stroke ET4. It was a great leap forward, or a great leap back, depending on one's viewpoint; indeed, the success of the model was arguably predicated on Piaggio's revived appreciation of its products as style items. After a decade or more of both short- and long-lived designs (each with their own committed fan bases) that were either too square-edged – the likes of the Cosa or even the much-loved PX – or rather old-fashioned looking – including the so-called New Line models launched in 1978 – the ET series finally struck the perfect balance. It was retro rather than retrospective, forward-looking without being futuristic, with curves in all the right places.

The ET4 might justifiably be credited with introducing the idea of scootering – or at least the Vespa marque – to a whole new generation at a time when scootering had been lost to niche interests. Indeed, the ET4 and its ilk even appealed to those who had ridden the scooters of the 1950s and 60s, who were finding maintenance of their old models to be increasingly prohibitively expensive, their performance temperamental and the market for equally vintage (and affordable) scooters drying up, with prices escalating. This itself was in no small part due to the fact that wealthier, older, 'born again' riders were returning to scootering in order to relive their youth, and because, while Italy may have been awash with Vespas in particular, many had tens of thousands of miles on the clock and had not been best looked after.

This was a characteristic of the culture that fully realised the post-war scooter: that it was treated more as a cheap and plentiful mode of transport,

Opposite: the Vespa Piaggio ET4, one of a series of 4-stroke machines launched in the late 1990s.

Left: Different cultures have contrasting ideas about the loading of scooters and the necessity of helmets.

Below: The launch of the Vespa Granturismo in New York in 2003.

countries around the world. A ride-out around Turin that June turned out to be the biggest Vespa rally in the world, attracting some 5,000 Vespas.

How much had these numbers swollen over the previous years thanks to the introduction of the ET4? Or to the trend for retro models that the ET4 had inspired, with manufacturers producing style rides with more than a hint of the 1950s and 60s to them – Piaggio included with its ET follow-up line, the LX of 2005 – with flowing lines and lots of chrome?

designed to be ridden into the ground and replaced, rather than as an artefact to be cherished and rarely used. Revealingly, the very first Vespa Club was founded in Saarbrucken, Germany, in 1951, triggering a wave that saw some 50,000 Vespa club members worldwide by the middle of the 1950s.

Come Vespa's 60th birthday in 2006, Piaggio had underscored this revival with the Granturismo, or GTL for short, and – driving the point that style mattered home – the GTV, or Granturismo Vintage, styled after models of the 1950s. Those niche interests were still in force though: the 2006 meeting of Eurovespa, the international Vespa rally, held in Italy, attracted some 3,000 'Vespisti' from 20

ADI CLARK
the custom scooter engraver

Adi Clark grew up listening to his mother's Trojan Reggae and dirt-tracking on his brother's Lambretta Jet 200. So it was perhaps inevitable the way his working life might go, After discovering the late 1970s Mod/Two Tone scene while living in Germany, a move to near Belfast didn't dint his style tendencies. On leaving school for a job in the NAAFI, supply services to the British military, he completed his mod uniform with his own scooter purchase. His real revelation came in the 1980s though, by when he was working his NAAFI contacts to secure a supply of army issue combat pants, which he passed on to the scooter boys in his scooter club.

'It was at the same time while I was rising over to the mainland UK rallies that I noticed some of the show-winning scooters having parts professionally decorated,' he says. 'I thought 'I got an art qualification at school', so I bought myself a spray gun and airbrush and tried my hand at it – but i had to admit I was I was too heavy-handed for painting murals. But I did notice engraving was slowly creeping on to the custom scene, so I took that up, never realising it would become my profession.'

Back on the British mainland and after a spell of factory work – with engraving proving a release in his spare time – Clark finally went into business with ACE (Adi Clark Engraving). He quickly rose to become one of the most respected custom engravers in the country – which is impressive given that he was self-taught.

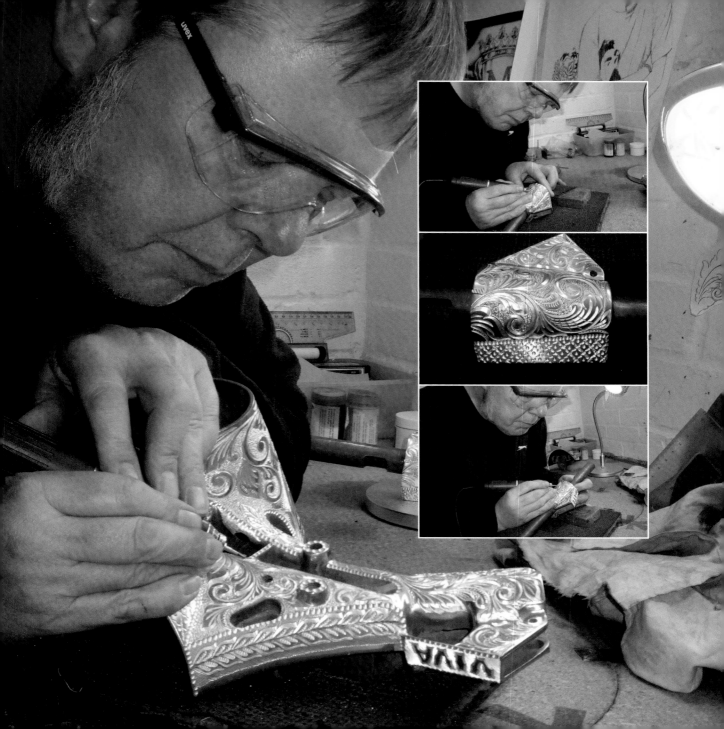

'Working in paint on a scooter you can, if it comes to it, go over a part and do the work again,' he notes. 'With engraving you have one go and one go only – it can be rather daunting at times especially if you're working on some rare original part that the scooter's owner has taken an age and spent good money to source. Engraving is all about the angle of the cuts you make, and how they catch the light. Go in at the wrong angle and engraving can look very flat. After that you learn by trial and error.' Clark will engrave what is known as 'scroll', 'script' and 'leaf-work', but notes that the client's choice of engraving can at times be ill-fitting to the scooter's actual theme, conceived, as it should be, as part of the whole scooter.

'Basic work can be done by an engraving machine but the reason the best custom engraved scooters are admired is because the work is a one-off, with a distinctive character and style,' Clark argues. 'Often first-timers to engraving come with ideas that can be too simple to be effective. I can't get excited by just wanting 'MODS' engraved somewhere on a scooter. But once I explain what is possible, to build their confidence, then the ideas take off. They might incorporate images and quotes from a theme, blending in scrollwork; their engraved surfaces become an extension to the theme of their custom painted bodywork. You want the client to be blown away by the final piece. And I'm interested in doing more complex pieces because my last job is my latest advertisement.'

The process is similar for every job: the parts to be engraved are polished to a mirror finish, to remove the bumps and bubbles on their surfaces (a product of the fact that many scooter parts are sand cast); the engraving follows. Clark draws on the basic design, focusing first on the main image and then completing the frame work around it by eye and hand. Finally, the parts are nickel-coated and plated by specialists, typically in chrome, gold, copper, bronze, a coating being required to protect the engraving (leaving the steel bare means the work will inevitably tarnish, with the necessary repeated polishing only then slowly degrading the work anyway).

The metals engraved mainly consist of Piaggio and Innocenti's original alloy and mild steel as they were cast in the factories. But supply and demand of hard to source parts has led these to be mass-produced using inferior metals; these are, Clark notes, fine for replacement and restoration work but not ideal for engraving. They make his skill all the more necessary.

'Most of my work is done on 1960s/70s Lambrettas and on 1980s/90s Vespas,' Clark says. 'People generally aren't aware of how much work goes into their engraving; they think you just pop the scooter part on a machine and press a button. A Vespa hub, for example, if detailed might actually require 10—15 hours engraving work, a chain-casing much more, maybe 26 hours' worth. They tend to be very surprised by the reality.'

While Clark has engraved everything from paisley patterns to Egyptian hieroglyphics – wittily, on closer inspection, blended into a psychedelic Beatles montage covering an entire Vespa PX – his specialism is challenging figurative work: portraying an individual, sometimes iconic, sometimes personal. 'Faces are difficult because a likeness really has to be true,' he says. 'I've done everyone from Marilyn Monroe to Paul Weller, Winston Churchill to the England 1966 World Cup squad; I have Morrissey emblazoned one of my own personal scooters.'

Much more trickily, he has also done people closer to home. 'With one job my client wanted an image of his wife engraved on a scooter casing, but in more 1950s Betty Paige style,' recalls Clark. 'So the customer took loads of photos of his wife for me to work from and I drew out the initial image. Next thing I knew I had his wife on the phone to me, ranting: 'You think I look like that?!' … Eventually she conceded that it was actually a very accurate drawing, just too accurate for her – so I ended up tweaking the image to reflect the way she looked when she was closer to 20 – none of the wrinkles, with a new hairstyle and a boob job. They loved it, as did I – though by then it really looked nothing like her.'

Malaguti even acknowledged the influence of nostalgia in the naming of one of its most successful models, the Yesterday. How much could be credited to the widespread standardisation of twist-and-go models, with belt-driven CVT (continuously variable transmission) giving riders maximum control over their scooter simply by using the throttle?

But, unlike the 1950s and 60s, Vespa was now by no means the leading light of the scooter scene. Scooter nerds and Mod revivalists may have preferred the brand, with a demand for fully restored vintage models ever present. But as much as scootering had new tribes, so, too, it had new icons,

with the ET4 seeing competition. The Velocifero was one new upstart of the 1990s. Launched by the relatively small company Italjet in 1993, somewhat out of left field, it had tiny wheels, a tiny engine and a pressed-steel-section chassis. But it also looked more retro than any of the models tapping into that aesthetic at the time, close, indeed, to D'Ascanio's very first Vespa. Its uptake by pop stars – the always Mod-inflected Oasis in the UK, REM in the US, not to mention the commissioning of shoe-designer Patrick Cox to create a limited-edition model – ensured that the Velocifero was unquestionably the coolest scooter of the next few years.

Opposite:
Mechanics fix old
Vespas in Ho Chi
Minh City,
Vietnam in 2005.

Below left:
Immaculate
vintage Vespas
and Lambrettas
with custom detail.

Below right:
A Velocifero
scooter parked at
Cefalu in Sicily.

Indeed, its apron and floorboard – the
characteristics that gave it its old-time scooter feel
– were supplied by Bajaj, the Indian company and
former manufacturing partner of Piaggio, and grafted
onto a tubular steel frame. Its 50cc engine, initially
regarded by many established scooterists as woefully
underpowered – it was, after all, half the size of the
very first Vespa – proved more than adequate given
advances in engine design and the lightness of
bodywork. In fact, 50cc models would soon come to
account for an estimated three-quarters of all
scooters sold, in part, perhaps, because (depending
on regulations nation to nation) the engine size made

CRAIG VETTER
the experimenter

Craig Vetter's first brush with scooters was helping his dad refurbish used scooters. He cleaned and sanded the wheels on a Cushman and painted them red for his dad to sell on to an American market hungry for these runabouts. 'But there was a designer in me then,' he says. 'I could see the structure of these scooters but always wanted them to have a more modern-looking bodywork – which I then made out of chicken wire and papier-mâché. And, no, it doesn't work.'

But despite his college days of the 1960s being populated with scooters – 'there was no snickering at anyone on a scooter,' he remembers, 'motorcycles may be more part of the American image but even then they were considered loud and dirty by my generation especially' – it wasn't until the Honda 50 arrived on the US market that his eyes were opened. 'By then I was riding a Vespa. When I saw the Honda I knew it was history in the making,' he adds. 'It was quiet, and easy to ride with those big wheels. There were no oil spills and it was, as scooters had promised to be, simple and hugely economical. I got rid of my Vespa.'

As heretical as that decision may be to many scooterists, it was that Honda model which turned Vetter on to his real interest: how to make two-wheeled transport more efficient, and this long before the idea of 'green' motoring was widely appreciated. The result? Inspired by his mentor, the legendary designer Buckminster Fuller – who Vetter would see lecture and occasionally chat with about his ideas – he began to design motorcycle fairings, and this while still a

design student undergraduate. 'My first love was always airplanes, so I was fascinated by aerodynamics – and I knew about fibreglass. In fact, I still have a piece I'd been given at a Corvette expo I went to when I was 10. So designing motorcycle fairings seemed like a good idea,' he explains.

And it was a hugely successful one. Adhering to one of Vetter's principles of good design – 'that something can't be more trouble than it's worth' – he created fairings that were light, affordable and simple to fit, and from the late 1960s to the late 1970s his business became the second biggest motorcycle-related company in the US, second only to the mighty Harley-Davidson. It was in 1978 that he decided to get out of the industry, disillusioned by its shift towards ever more unnecessarily powerful, gas-guzzling motorcycles; the opposite, indeed, of what the scooter had promised.

'By then, cars were starting to offer better fuel economy than some motorcycles of the time,' he notes. 'I was embarrassed by what my fellow motocyclists were doing. It went against my goal of doing more with less, in my case trying to produce transport that went further with less.'

That led him to investigations into streamlining, which he first experimented with by chopping back a Kawasaki and making it more aerodynamic – giving it an unprecedented 107mpg – as well as by launching a national competition to provide improved miles per gallon at legal speed limits. 'The realisation was that, taking lessons from scooter design, streamlining everything does give better performance – you get more with less,' says Vetter. 'Streamlining

has only one shape – rounded at the front, pointed at the rear and with the smallest cross section the rider can fit into. Scooters, with their 'step through seating', lend themselves to those principles.'

It wasn't until 1998 that the vehicles that followed these principles and for which he is best known in the scooter world came about. One was the Torpedo, an exercise in streamline styling, 'and with every design cliché of the 50s on it too,' Vetter adds, 'from tail fins to port holes to two-tone paintwork. It wasn't really serious. It was the retro style but exaggerated, yet resulted in one heck of a scooter.' His other design, however, was much more serious. He took a Honda Helix and effectively redesigned its exterior to boost its streamlining and, again, built up a successful business selling, in kit form, what he dubbed the Helix Streamliner.

'I stripped it down and streamlined it and, you know what, it works and works better,' explains Vetter. 'A Helix typically won't go at 70mph into a 30mph head wind carrying four bags of groceries. Mine will. With no change at all to the engine my Helix will do 100mpg in those same conditions. That's double what a standard Helix scooter will. So it seems that now I'm back on a scooter.'

Will Vetter's approach be of influence? One wonders if the scooter industry may in years to come look on Vetter as some kind of visionary in this field, much like his mentor. 'No manufacturers seem to care about streamlining. I guess people think it looks odd. But if energy ever becomes precious we will all want to be streamlined,' predicts Vetter. 'Styling is great, but it has to do more than look good. It has to help people live better, which, after all, is why we like scooters.'

Below: Honda
Scoopys for rent
to tourists at
Ayutthaya in
Thailand.

Opposite: The
Italjet Torpedo is
a hybrid between
a scooter and a
motorcycle.

them accessible both to younger riders and those who had been banned from riding anything bigger. In some parts of the US 50cc models were known cheekily as 'liquor cycles'.

This best of both worlds format certainly worked for the American market, its scooter scene by then dominated by Japanese models, the distribution of European brands effectively non-existent and the prices of vintage scooters rocketing. The Velocifero, in fact, was the first Italian scooter available in the US since the Vespa P series in 1977, so was destined to prove as big a hit there as it already was in Europe.

Perhaps its only rivals were the new big-wheeled scooters that also became something of a faddish hit over the same period. The likes of the Honda Scoopy, Piaggio Peperino and Liberty, Italjet's own Torpedo and, most successfully, Aprilia's Scarabeo 50 – set to become one of the bestselling scooters of all time – offered a similar retro-futuristic style but with more stability and easier handling, factors that appealed to the teen market. The Scarabeo was influential in shaping demand for scooters in the bigger picture, too. Its impressive sales figures have in part been attributed to Aprilia's determination to sell through scooter-only dealerships, a number of which

consequently opened for business. It seemed that, rather than attempt to sell scooters alongside motorbikes, as their poor country cousins, a scooter-only environment was better able to sell to scooter-minded customers.

Piaggio was also quick to capitalise on this new interest in scootering, turning what had, from the 1950s through to the 1970s, been a more

COLIN SHATTUCK

the dealer

Colin Shattuck worked at a motorcycle dealership during which time a love of ska music re-introduced him to scooters. It chimed with something that had been with him since a child. 'I remember as a kid always imagining having this personal vehicle that was just mine and shaped like a Tylenol capsule – something small and very futuristic – and one day I caught a flash of a Lambretta in a movie. And that was it for me,' he says.

Seeing one in the metal, so to speak, was enough to make him switch from the big machines. 'After all,' he says, 'speed is such a relative thing. At 45mph around town you still feel like you're really moving just as fast as you are doing 95mph on a big bike on the highway, but you have all that shiny metalwork and style beneath you. At the time of my first scooter I also had a 750cc Kawasaki, and when I wasn't getting speeding tickets I was lumbering around on it. I still love motorcycles. But of the 14 or so vehicles I have in my garage right now, the ones that will start are all scooters.'

But without a network of scooter enthusiasts or a scooter scene to speak of at the time – this was the early 1990s – it was his work at the motorcycle dealership that actually persuaded him he could turn a newfound passion into a business. 'It was around 1992 and I was parking my Vespa outside the dealership, and it seemed like more people were coming in to ask me about that than to buy a motorcycle,' he recalls. 'So I thought if I could buy a couple of scooters I could flip them and make some money. Finding them was all through word of mouth or the occasional classified ad in the

paper. It wasn't easy then. But the writing was on the wall: the more I sold, the more people then needed servicing or repairs, and the more scooters were in demand.'

Shattuck launched his dealership Sportique Scooters in Denver, Colorado, in 1998, with subsequent branches opening across the state. But he puts the real forward motion of his business over the following years down to a handful of models, and none of them Vespas, this in large part due to the politically complex mismanagement of the brand as a lifestyle product in the US over that period. The first was the Italjet Velocifero – not least because Sportique secured an order of 18 of the scooters from haircare company American Crew, which wanted them as sales incentives for its retailers. 'We couldn't get hold of enough of them fast enough,' Shattuck says. 'It wasn't that the Velocifero was anything special at the time – although in retrospect it probably was – so much as it was so unlike any other option: it really evoked that Italian flair. There was no way Vespa would ever have come back to the US and found a market here without the Velocifero. It turned the scooter market on in the US.'

The second was the Aprilia Scarabeo, both for its distinctive looks and ease of riding – 'we beat the door down at Aprilia to get hold of those, and became one of the few scooter-only Aprilia dealerships in the country,' says Shattuck – but also because Aprilia's sales support, and the launch of the first scooter dealer conventions, allowed connections to be made and a bona fide scooter industry in the US to grow for the first time since the 1960s. Sportique's other key models have included the Scarabeo-like Kymko People and the Genuine Buddy – 'small, easy to operate, high-quality machines made for urban people,' as Shattuck puts it.

Not that life as a scooter dealer has been without its troughs. Shattuck recalls what initially looked to be the boom time of 2008, for example, when petrol prices in the US rocketed and the emphasis for scooters 'switched from being about style and fun and about offering economy,' he says. 'There was actually a scooter shortage, so many were being sold. I had an empty showroom. But that only encouraged many dealers to over-order for 2009 – just in time for an economic crisis. It was a bloodbath: over half of all scooter dealerships in the US closed. It was a thinning of the herd, and probably good in the long run. We survived by fixing scooters. We'd sold enough that we had a good serving business.'

Other lows came with the rise of knock-off scooters imported from China that, Shattuck says, had a cheap enough ticket price to tempt many customers away from quality products: 'Enthusiasts who know and care about scooter history are a small but critical part of the scene, but most customers don't give a crap about history,' he adds. 'Fortunately markets learn and steer again towards better quality.' And then, perhaps inevitably, to return to that national love of big motorcycles, there is the enduring image problem for scooters in the US.

'There is a growing appreciation for that European sense of style and quality here that works for the scooter market, but then we also have monster trucks and NASCAR [National Association for Stock Car Racing],' Shattuck jokes. 'There is still the wide perception that scooters are for pussies, or at least there is outside of metropolitan centers. The closer you are to a cosmopolitan city, the less likely a scooter will be thought of as something for girls. But, no doubt, if you're in one of those cities, scooters have a certain cool.'

The opening of
a new Vespa
boutique in New
York in 2002.

underground appreciation into a no-holds-barred lifestyle and style choice – a designer brand of sorts. A huge range of colour options was launched – far greater than anything rival companies could offer – accessories were plentiful and Piaggio revived its tried-and-tested marketing formula of product placement. Vespa boutiques opened across Europe and the US, selling everything from Vespa-branded all-weather jackets, to T-shirts, watches and even soaps. The experiment was only half successful, not least because Piaggio chose not to make the products available to dealerships selling non-Piaggio products. But it did suggest that the view of scooters as a style statement had gone mainstream.

Tellingly, the Japanese manufacturers were soon producing new larger-wheeled and better styled scooters of their own: the Yamaha Vino of 2001 and the Honda Metro of the following year were among the best and, in part because of their makers' huge distribution networks, were – like the Honda Cub before – soon massive sellers. Not that the Japanese makers would stop with mere imitation.

Yes, there is some truth that it was attempting to do this in its motorcycle industry at the time, aiming to reproduce the big American styling and sound of the Harley Davidson. But its scooter industry saw an opportunity for innovation, or at least to reintroduce the idea German scooter manufacturers had pioneered back in the 1950s: the 'maxi' scooter was a tourer, large-engined, comfortable and with spacious storage, easily capable of travel between towns and, on some models, of getting between them at well over 100mph. These new scooters appealed to riders for whom perhaps a touring motorcycle remained too large, too heavy, too dirty, too expensive. One of the early designs in the category, the Honda CH125 Spacy, launched in 1983, even returned to the promise made by those larger scooters of the 1950s: that it was more car-like. Yes, the Spacy had a foot-level heater.

The timing must have seemed right: Honda went on to launch its ground-breaking, space-age Helix, the 'commuter scooter', in 1986 to disappointing sales, despite even more car-like qualities – floor-mats, a full dashboard and the like – and despite its uptake by wealthy customers with an eye for a progressive automotive benchmark. Unfortunately, there were just not enough of them; so disappointing were the sales, in fact, that the company dropped it within a year. It was relaunched, unchanged, seven years later,

MARCO LAMBRI

the designer

Marco Lambri has his dream job. 'I was working for the design centre at Alfa Romeo, but during the evenings and at the weekends I designed motorbikes and scooters,' he says. 'They were my real passion.' That's unsurprising given that his father ran a small workshop, and that Lambri was given his first scooter at the age of 8. 'But I loved motorbikes more then,' he concedes. 'I was young and was attracted to performance. In fact, the only scooter that really interested me was the Vespa, and I soon got into tweaking the performance on those and making changes to the body work to 'improve' them.'

Clearly this did not count against him: Lambri joined Piaggio in 2004, rising to become its head of design. He developed the company's LX line, as well as its S series and V series, chiefly as a means of giving Piaggio's range an aesthetic definition along 'sport' and 'vintage' – the two chief scootering camps, as Piaggio sees it. 'When we design we have to be conscious of the fact that the same scooter is responded to in very different ways around the world,' Lambri stresses. 'In India, for example, there is no appreciation of the scooter as having 'retro' appeal. In fact, there it's perceived as being a poor man's vehicle. They want motorbikes. And it's different again in Italy, where we grow up surrounded by scooters. And image changes. When I was growing up there wasn't much of an appreciation of a scooter as a style item – but that is more the case now. Now they launch new, locally made scooters in Asia, for example, by talking up the fact that they have been 'styled in Italy'.'

Appealing to international markets is only one of Lambri's considerations when designing a new model, a process that can take some 18 months from first sketch to working prototype. He and his team work closely with Piaggio's commercial departments in identifying new markets, developing a brief and then making propositions to answer that brief.

'We use 3D-computer aided design systems to represent the final shape of the new scooter, and when we present an innovative idea to focus groups the reaction is usually bad,' admits Lambri. 'But that's OK. The customer is typically very conservative so we in design have to convince those in marketing that getting a positive response in focus groups isn't good for us – it means the idea we've proposed is probably an old one.' The design process will go on to create several 1:1 scale models, using plastics and clay, 'because you still really need a physical mock-up – it's hard to convince anyone when they can't see a 'real' scooter in front of them,' Lambri adds. 'Then, just when you think the design work is over, we start fighting with the engineering department, over the costs of components, for example. We often say that the job of the design department is to encourage engineering to adopt a similar approach to innovation.'

Lambri is, of course, always thinking way ahead as to how the next generation of scooters might perform, what they might look like, what innovations they might embody. He notes, for example, how the physical relationship between a car and its driver is very different to that between a scooter and its rider. 'You have to ride a scooter with your whole body, and that has a major impact on ergonomics,' says Lambri. One likely area of development for the future is, he says, a means of adjusting the riding position for a

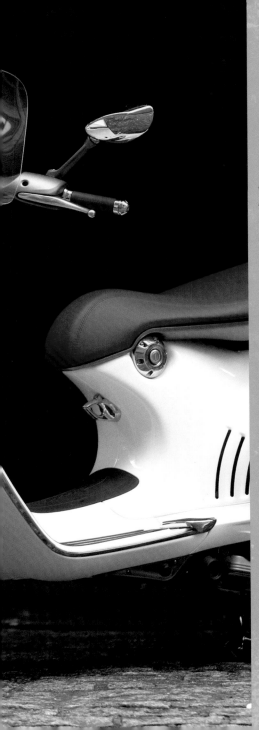

more tailored fit to the rider, 'so the same model works for the tall rider in Scandinavia as the short rider in Vietnam,' he jokes. Anyone who dismissed the BMW C1 as something of a gimmick might be shocked by Lambri's other predictions: 'We will see scooters of more diversity, somewhere between the scooter we know now and an electric bicycle, for example. We will see scooters with airbags and,' he says, 'scooters with roofs. That's the next major step – like the C1 but without its stability problems. All such developments could transform the aesthetic of the scooter altogether.'

And it is not just the way that scooters look that is set to change radically, Lambri suggests. Our whole attitude to what they represent, what they are for and how they fit into increasingly urbanized living will also change the scooter over the coming decades in ways that Piaggio's founder could not have imagined.

'Generally scooters are often perceived as being functional first, and less about the aesthetic – most people just use them to get about easily and inexpensively. But I'm not sure that is so true today as more and more people consider the scooter both as something that could work for them, and in the same aesthetic terms most people might think of a car,' says Lambri. 'Cars are increasingly anachronistic – if you're sat in one alone you're moving metal and air. You don't need all that volume most of the time. So I think the future of mobility if likely to tend towards some kind of vehicle part way between a car and a scooter. The scooter, the Vespa especially, may represent Italian style. But the big question is how to interpret its characteristics to meet the needs of modern city living as it will be. We're just at the beginning of a revolution in transport.'

again to no great acclaim. And then launched again, in 2004, some 18 years after its first appearance. This time it could ride the zeitgeist it had been so far ahead of for so long.

By this time it had been joined by the likes of the Honda Reflex 250, Honda Silverwing 600 and aptly named Honda Foresight, the Piaggio Hexagon and Yamaha Majesty. Tellingly the Majesty was a bestseller for two years in, of all places, Italy. Aprilia's Atlantic was aptly named, too, being almost as big as

its namesake. It had over 45 litres of under-seat storage space, more than some sports cars of the time. In their longer form and boxier bodies, there was something futuristic about the style of these scooters, a style which marked a departure from the curvy classics of yesteryear and suggested the ride of tomorrow. The Suzuki Burgman 650 and 400 perhaps did this best. Most curious, however, was BMW's C1, a scooter with seat belt, stereo system, mobile phone charger, huge luggage capacity and,

Opposite: Suzuki's 400cc Burgman 400Z, one of a new breed of larger scooters.

Left: A rally of BMW C1s in support of not wearing helmets while riding this unusual bike.

most striking of all, a crash-tested roof that meant riders in Germany were exempted from wearing a helmet. Perhaps this, like so many scooter designs before, was an idea before its time, perhaps its looks were just too quirky, or perhaps it was simply too expensive, but the C1 was not the success that BMW had hoped for.

The sheer variety available in the maxi scooter sector had, regardless, proven that transport's scooter category still had room for both new possibilities and a wider audience. Small wonder then that Chinese (as well as Taiwanese and Vietnamese) manufacturers wanted to jump on the opportunity by launching their own, much cheaper alternatives. And they did so with all guns blazing: over the first four years of the 2000s, some 20 different scooter brands emerged out of China, among them Taizhou Kaitong, Zhejiang, Geeley and Qingpi. Most were obviously mechanically substandard quality compared with the European and Japanese models from which they liberally borrowed their styling cues.

In fact, most were sold on a grey market basis and, since they did not meet many national regulations, were also sold as being for 'off-road use only', despite that clearly not being the intention of

middle men and end customers alike. For a time Chinese scooters found their way to the US via a mass-market retailer – akin to the earlier introduction of Vespa and other leading makes through catalogue companies Sears and Montgomery Wards – this time the discount, members-only operation Costco.

Tourers were not, however, the only option of this later scooter renaissance. What better alternative to the heavy, long-distance machine than one that seemed almost disposable in its low power, low cost and lower quality build? Piaggio had a hit with its Skipper, but again it was the Japanese who produced these brightly coloured, plastic-bodied twist-and-go 'pop' models, the likes of Yamaha's BW – the 'B-whizz' as it was dubbed – which introduced yet another generation to the joys of two-wheeled mobility, one free of the cultural baggage of yesteryear. Indeed, the global scooter market would soon become dominated by Japanese companies, notably after they bought up struggling European manufacturers such as Spain's Montesa – acquired by Honda – and France's Motobecane – acquired by Yamaha. Only Piaggio remained as a serious European contender. For many, that was what it always had been.

Index

Credits

The publishers are grateful to the following photographers for permission to reproduce their images: **2** Ed Keogh/Alamy; **4** Dmitri KesselThe LIFE Picture Collection/Getty; **6** Lyndon McNeil; **8** Nik Wheeler/Alamy; **10** Andrew Cowie/Stringer/Getty; **12** Francesco Iacobelli/JAI/Corbis; **14** Hedda Gjerpen/Getty; **15** Library of Congress; **16** SSPL/Getty; **18l** Lordprice Collection/Alamy; **18r** Mary Evans Picture Library; **19** Mortons Archive; **20** Corbis; **22** John Kobal Foundation Moviepix/Getty; **23t** Motoring Picture Library/Alamy; **23b** Mortons Archive; **24** Lambretta Museum; **25** Lambretta Museum; **26** Keystone-France Gamma-Keystone/Getty; **27** David Lees/Corbis; **28** Mortons Archive; **30** Mortons Archive; **31** Motoring Picture Library/Alamy; **32** Dmitri Kessel The LIFE Picture Collection; **33** Express Hulton Archive/Getty; **35t** Reporters Associes, Gamma-Rapho/Getty; **35b** James Whitmore, The LIFE Images Collection/Getty; **37t, 37c, 37b** Lambretta Museum; **38-41** Lyndon McNeil; **42** Mortons Archive; **43** Mondadori/Getty; **44** Popperfoto/Getty; **45** Bettmann/Corbis; **46** Lambretta Museum; **47** Mortons Archive; **49** Jacobsen Hulton Archive/Getty; **50** Lambretta Museum; **51** The Enthusiast Network/Getty; **53** Nina Leen, The LIFE Premium Collection/Getty; **54** Mortons Archive; **55** John Sunderland Denver Post/Getty; **56** Bettmann/Corbis; **57l** Motoring Picture Library/Alam; **57r** Roger Viollet/Topfoto; **58** Mortons Archive; **59t** Lambretta Museum; **59b** Mortons Archive; **60** Keystone-France Gamma-Keystone/Getty; **63** Lambretta Museum; **64** Harry Kerr Hulton Archive/Getty; **65** Motoring Picture Library/Alamy; **67t** Lambretta Museum; **67c** Lambretta Museum; **67b** Dave King/Getty; **68** Terry Fincher Hulton Archive/Getty; **70** Lambretta Museum; **71** Lambretta Museum;

72 Lambretta Museum; **73r** Apic Hulton Archive/Getty; **74** AF archive/Alamy; **76l** Bettmann/Corbis; **76r** Mortons Archive; **77** Alinari Archives/Corbis; **78** Mortons Archive; **79** Popperfoto/Getty; 80-85 Lyndon McNeil; **86** David Redfern/Getty; **87** Mortons Archive; **89** Keystone-France Gamma-Keystone/Getty; **91** Curbishley-Baird/The Kobal Collection; **92** Mortons Archive; **95b** Mortons Archive; **95t** Mortons Archive; **96-99** Lyndon McNeil; **101tl** Mortons Archive; **101tr** Keystone-France Gamma-Keystone/Getty; **101bl** John Dominis The LIFE Picture Collection/Getty; **101br** Mortons Archive; **102** Mortons Archive; **104-109** Lyndon McNeil; 110 Bruno Vincent Getty Images News/Getty; **111** PYMCA Universal Images Group/Getty; **112r** Dan Kitwood Getty Images News/Getty; **113** Sinister Pictures/Demotix/Corbis; **114-117** Paddy Smith; **119** Keystone-France Hulton Archive/Getty; **120-125** Lyndon McNeil; **126** Mortons Archive; **129** Lyndon McNeil; **130-133** Lyndon McNeil; **134** American Stock Archive Archive Photos/Getty; **135** FPG Archive Photos/Getty; **136** Lenscap/Alamy; **139b** Neil Setchfield/Alamy; **139tl** Mortons Archive; **139tr** Mortons Archive; **140-143** Lyndon McNeil; **144** Malcolm Fairman/Alamy; **145t** Mark Bassett/Alamy; **145c** Nik Wheeler/Alamy; **145br** J. Countess WireImage/Getty; **146-149** Adi Clark; **150** Hoang Dinh Nam AFP/Getty; **151t** Lenscap/Alamy; **151b** FirstShot/Alamy; **152-155** Craig Vetter; **156** LG Anderson/Alamy; **157** Simon Evans/Alamy; **158-161** Joe Amon Denver Post/Getty; **162** Matthew Peyton Getty Images Entertainment/Getty; **164-165** Marco Lambri; **167** Bloomberg; **168** Imagebroker/Alamy; **169** Ian Miles-Flashpoint Pictures/Alamy; **174** Lyndon McNeil; **176** Mortons Archive.